"This is one of the best curricula I've seen for facilitating social and emotional development for youth. Students experience transformations in self-awareness, acquire practical tools for effective communication and problem-solving, and develop genuine connection to their community."

—NANCY SCHIFF, EXECUTIVE DIRECTOR FOR

THE CENTER FOR YOUTH DEVELOPMENT THROUGH LAW

"The teachings in this soulful, systematic sourcebook will plant the seeds of empathy and empowerment in any classroom. Jackson knows and honors adolescence: her accessible designs for community-building and conversation create space for teenagers to walk their paths with purpose and awareness."

—MELINA CENTOMANI RUTTER, SAN LORENZO, CALIFORNIA,

HIGH SCHOOL TEACHER

"Jackson's practical ideas for promoting self-awareness, empathy, social engagement, and mindfulness are diverse enough to appeal to all kinds of girls and their mentors and parents. This is a powerful resource for both secular organizations and religious communities to use in making a real difference in girls' lives."

—THE REV. DR. KAREN MARIE YUST, *REAL KIDS, REAL FAITH*,

ROWE PROFESSOR OF CHRISTIAN EDUCATION,

UNION PRESBYTERIAN SEMINARY

"*Girls Rising* is not only a well-researched, engaging program of action to support and guide girls as they navigate the harrowing complexities of adolescence. It is a poignant exhortation to tend to the souls of our girls so that they will be better equipped to fight for what is good and right in the world—beginning with themselves."

—JUNGWON KIM, SENIOR EDITORIAL MANAGER OF
THE RAINFOREST ALLIANCE, MOTHER OF TEEN GIRLS

"With beautiful eloquence, Urana Jackson has managed to finally give voice to the personal, social, and spiritual development of the adolescent girl. Where can I sign my clients and daughter up?"

— NATALIA EL-SHEIKH, MARRIAGE AND FAMILY THERAPIST

"As a director of programs for a mental health agency, I am so grateful for this collection of activities for young women that Urana has put together. *Girls Rising* offers a comprehensive and deeply moving curriculum that can be used to help girls develop into strong and insightful women."

—LILY LY, PHD

Girls RISING

Girls
RISING

A GUIDE TO NURTURING A CONFIDENT
AND SOULFUL ADOLESCENT

Urana Jackson

PARALLAX
PRESS

Berkeley, California

Parallax Press

P.O. Box 7355

Berkeley, California 94707

parallax.org

Parallax Press is the publishing division of Unified Buddhist Church, Inc.

Cover and text design by Nancy Austin

Cover image © iStock/stellalevi

Author photo © Rhythm Krishna Mohan

All other photography © Rhythm Krishna Mohan

Feelings Worksheet artwork on p. 67 © Nina Soberanis

Illustration on p. 65 © arlatis/Shutterstock

Illustration on p. 160 © MARK-N/Shutterstock

Printed on 100% post-consumer waste recycled paper

Library of Congress Cataloging-in-Publication Data is available upon request

ISBN: 978-1-941529-18-8

1 2 3 4 5 / 20 19 18 17 16

Girl Rising

After the gossamer veil of childhood has lifted

Ash and shadow spill out and

The numbing starts to quicken

While in small, heart-opening moments

When she is wild, and blind, and perfectly broken

She begins to understand that

Her gut isn't something to suck in, but to listen to.

Baring her heart unshielded is an act that both unifies and liberates, and

Beauty is not a vacant image that is erected—

Rather it is a goddess-given right that you grow into

Slowly

From the inside

Then

She begins to rise

Like the dawn

She stretches out and connects to the Beloved World

Touching another Self

Which she has only yet to realize.

—Urana Jackson

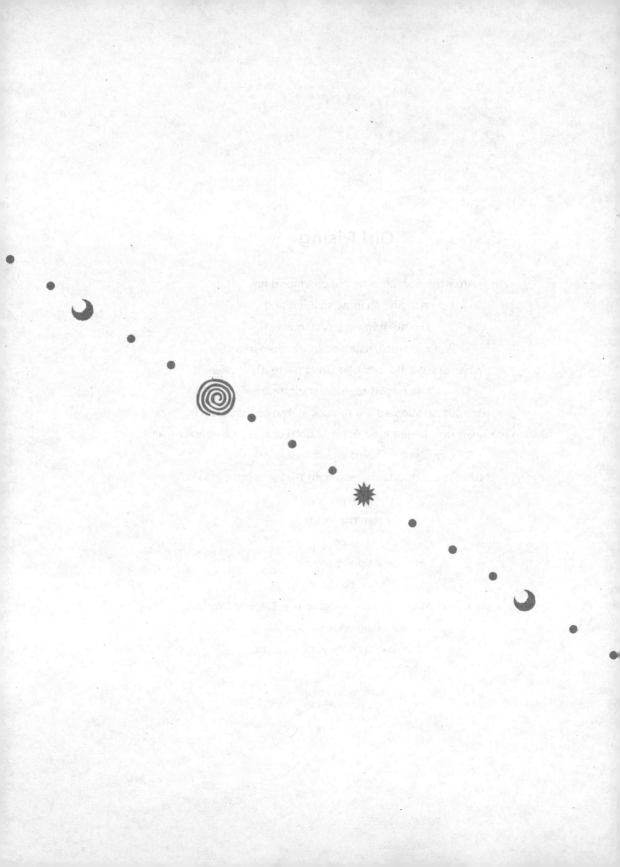

Contents

Introduction

Girls in Hiding

I began my work with girls when I was twenty-six. I was a young woman myself, still wrestling with old ghosts of self-worth and identity, as a biracial female navigating my place between a wealthy white community and middle-lower income black community; as an only child from a single-parent home; and as an extremely sensitive soul trying to make my way through the assaulting environment of Los Angeles in the 1980s. I was seeking the very empowerment that I was expected to offer the girls I was mentoring. It is no coincidence that people enter into this work as therapists, educators, and advocates with their own wounds. The ways in which we heal from them are reflected by and conducted through those people and issues we serve. As the Eastern saying quoted by Eckhart Tolle in *The Power of Now: a Guide to Spiritual Enlightenment* goes, "The teacher and the taught together create the teaching."

My work with girls first began at an afterschool program in San Francisco public housing; three years later I moved to the girls' unit at a juvenile detention center; and then, beginning in 2001, I spent thirteen years working in Oakland public schools. The young women I worked with came from a broad range of racial, ethnic, and socioeconomic backgrounds. They were vibrant, intelligent, saucy, and creative, yet many of them, regardless of their backgrounds and personal attributes, were struggling desperately with issues of depression or anxiety, drug and/or alcohol abuse, social isolation, bulimia, anorexia, cutting, perfectionism, abusive relationships, and more. It seemed like, as a collective, these girls were going through an initiation through fire, and the institutions surrounding them were ill-equipped to provide a container for such a chaotic and soul-deep passage.

Like many service providers committed to understanding and impacting a particular issue, I began my process by asking some fundamental questions: What are the deeper, underlying issues at play? In girl-centered practices I have seen, what works and what doesn't work? What is not being addressed? How can I convey what I believe is needed in a manner that is authentic, innovative, and respectful of the populations I serve? What are my personal strengths and gifts, and how can they be employed here? It has taken more than seventeen years to answer these first questions. *Girls Rising* is my response to that inquiry.

One of the first components in my initial search was to understand the underlying factors affecting the girls I was working with. I sought out seminal works from feminist psychologists like Carol Gilligan, Lyn Mekel Brown, and Mary Pipher, who offered critical insight into the complexity of girls' development. I began to understand that at some point during the preteen years, many girls begin to lose their way, abandoning activities, beliefs, and relationships that were once life-affirming, and begin to doubt their choices, abilities, desires, and self-worth. This loss of self is evident in the myriad disturbing statistics about the psychological, emotional, and physical health of adolescent girls: seven out of ten girls ages thirteen to seventeen believe they "are not good enough" in regard to their looks, school performance, and relationships.[1] Girls are three times more likely to experience depression than their male counterparts.[2] Adolescent girls are more vulnerable to substance abuse and addiction, and are beginning to surpass adolescent boys in alcohol use.[3] Forty-two percent of first through third-grade girls wish they were thinner.[4] And according to research conducted by the Center for Disease Control (CDC), one in four young women report having been raped or sexually assaulted by the age of eighteen.[5]

....

1   Dove Real Girls, "Real Pressure: A National Report on the State of Self-Esteem." Dove.us/ Articles and Advice.

2   "Results from the 2010 national survey on drug use and health: National Findings Office of Applied Studies," Substance Abuse and Mental Health Services Administration. Series H-22, accessed November 2015, archive.samhsa.gov/data/NSDUH/2K10NSDUH/2K10Results.pdf

3   "The Formative Years: Pathways to Substance Abuse among Girls and Young Women Ages 8-22," National Center on Addiction and Substance Abuse (Washington, DC: February 5, 2003).

4   M.E. Collins, "Body figure perceptions and preferences among pre-adolescent children," *International Journal of Eating Disorders* 10 (March 1991): 199-208.

5   "Adverse Childhood Experiences Study: Data and Statistics," Center for Disease Control and Prevention, last modified May 13, 2014. http://www.cdc.gov/nccdphp/ace/prevalence.htm.

With the onset of puberty, girls and boys undergo hormonal changes that have a major impact on their psychological equilibrium. They experience these changes in a culture steeped in misogyny, materialism, and spiritual disconnection that casts its invisible hand via the media, advertising, and other avenues, and so a girl begins to suspect that in order to fit the culture's prescriptions of beauty and value, she may be unable to hold on to the person she knows herself to be. In response, she hides, surrenders, or rages in vain against these ubiquitous forces.

It is as the old fables prophesized: the princess succumbs to an evil curse and falls into everlasting sleep, or loses her voice, or gets impossibly lost in a forest and goes mad. The story usually concludes as the princess is brought back to life by a kiss from a prince, but we know a new narrative must emerge. In the new story, the princess's environment provides her with a safe space and a set of powerful psycho-spiritual tools so that she may find her way home, restore her own sanity, and wake herself up—to the powerful and embodied woman she is meant to be.

Initiation "Rights"

Many indigenous cultures have established some kind of "container," a psychological or spiritual space to both acknowledge and inform young people's transition into adulthood. This initiation or rite of passage offers a vehicle for the neophyte to learn profound lessons about themselves and the world around them, as well as to clarify and affirm their identity and role in the community. One can still see examples of these rites in hundreds of cultures around the world, including, for example, the Navajo Kinaalda ceremony, the Central and South American Quinceañera celebration, and the Maasai coming of age tradition in Tanzania and Kenya, to name only a few. I believe that these initiatory imprints remain embedded in the modern psyche because this transition is a necessary part of the human experience. Moreover, depth psychologist Richard Frankel states in his book *The Adolescent Psyche*, "If the archetype of initiation is a structural component of the psyche, then it is going to occur whether or not a given culture formally invests in such rites."[6]

....
6 Richard Frankel, *The Adolescent Psyche: Jungian and Winnicottian Perspectives* (London: Routledge, 1998).

While some cultural and religious communities provide transitional rites, American secular culture has very little to offer the deeper psychic needs of its young people, so often they create their own rite of passage. Because this self-initiation is entirely unconscious, and unsupported by either an initiated adult or the community in general, the passage is fraught with chaos and danger. Sometimes young people are unable to recover fully from such turbulent trials and instead are left with the devastating aftermath: unplanned pregnancies, drug and alcohol addiction, incarceration, and broken self-esteem—consequences that not only have long-term, destructive effects on individuals and their loved ones but that also contribute to the overall weakening of our shared social fabric.

With a near absence of any meaningful initiation into adulthood in the mainstream culture, alongside a cultural paradigm that derails female self-worth, it is essential that parents and guardians, schools, and communities be prepared to provide girls with an evocative and thoughtful process around their transition into womanhood. This process should be holistic in that it integrates psycho-emotional, social, and spiritual elements to address these young people's multifaceted natures. It should be done in a spirit of safety and respect, ultimately offering girls the *right* to define for themselves their own truth and meaning. Finally, this exploration should offer relevant and effective tools and perspectives that will help propel young women toward a greater sense of personal wholeness.

A Note on Spirituality in Youth Development

I define spirituality as the awareness of and search for connection with something greater than oneself, be it a set of values, a higher power, or transcendent experiences. For many people, the term "spirituality" is problematic. For some, it conjures impressions of mandalas or pulpits, fundamentalism or New Age movements, and many people are particularly careful about distancing spirituality from secular education and youth development in general. The First Amendment prohibits the imposition of any one religious practice or ideology in public schools, to ensure that public educational space is kept free from indoctrination, and as a result many young people's spiritual or religious education is relegated to their parents' contributions. This is limiting for at least two reasons. First, many parents or guardians fear the dogma and conditioning sometimes associated with religious and spiritual affiliation, and instead take a passive stance, providing little or no spiritual introduction or exposure to young people, imagining that their children will discover their spiritual identity, if any, when they become adults. However, it is precisely during the period of adolescence that an individual is most receptive to and perhaps in need of a spiritual outlook or philosophy. Second, parents who attend to their children's spiritual upbringing often do so by merely extending their own philosophy and practices. While this is understandable, one result is that young people may not get to explore what genuinely resonates with their own hearts and minds, instead adopting their parents' faith with a mechanical devotion that they often abandon as adults.[7]

Adolescence is a crucial stage for spiritual inquiry and development.[8] During adolescence, the mind begins to open to personal reflection and abstract thinking, including a spiritual conception of reality.[9] Teenagers begin to perceive the world through a wider, more sophisticated lens, which can be illuminating and electrifying. Young people are acutely aware of, and identify with, the main principle of spirituality in one form or another: a recent Gallup poll indicates that approximately 95 percent of American teenagers say that they believe in God or a higher power.[10] Moreover, a number of studies in the last ten years have linked an adolescent's connection to spiritual concepts with moral development, emotional regulation, life satisfaction, prosocial behaviors, and a successful transition

---

7   Pew Research Center, "Faith in Flux," 2009. Revised in 2011 (http://www.pewforum.org/2009/04/27/fath-in-flux/).

8   P. E. King and C. J. Boyatzis, "Exploring adolescent spiritual and religious development: current and future theoretical and empirical perspectives," *Applied Developmental Science Volume 8*, no. 1 (2004).
    P. L. Benson, E. C. Roehlkepartain, and S. P. Rude, "Spiritual development in childhood and adolescence: toward a field of inquiry," *Applied Developmental Science 7*, no. 3 (2003): 205–213.
    P. S. Y. Lau, "Spirituality as a positive youth development construct: conceptual bases and implications for curriculum development," *International Journal of Adolescent Medicine and Health* 18, no. 3 (2006).

9   D. Elkind, "The origins of religion in the child," *Review of religious research 12* (1970).

10 G. Gallup and R. Bezilla. *The Religious Life of Young Americans: A Compendium of Surveys on the Spiritual Beliefs and Practices of Teenagers and Young Adults* (Princeton, NJ: 1992).

to adulthood.[11] Educator and author Rachel Kessler further elucidates the need and benefits of a "soulful education":

> The body of the child will not grow if it is not fed; the mind will not flourish unless it is stimulated and guided. And the spirit will suffer if it is not nurtured. A soulful education embraces diverse ways to satisfy the spiritual hunger of today's youth. When guided to find constructive ways to express their spiritual longings, young people can find purpose in life, do better in school, strengthen ties to family and friends, and approach life with validity and vision.[12]

While there appears to be a developmental need for, a genuine interest in, and a favorable outcome to exposing youth to spiritual exploration and existential questions about themselves and the world around them, young people rarely get the opportunity to explicitly examine these questions, particularly in a space that is guided, impartial, exploratory, and inclusive. In most youth development work, this component has been almost completely overlooked.

In my experience as a therapist and an educator working with adolescents, the issue of spirituality comes up time and time again. Young people's questions are incessant: What happens when we die? Why do some good people die early and why do some bad people never face justice? What do my dreams mean? Why is there so much suffering in the world? Why are we here? In the beginning, I worried that fostering these existential discussions was inappropriate for a public-school setting and moreover was off-topic, so I would eventually lead the discussion back to the intended theme. However, over time I began to allow space for the discussion to evolve, and what I experienced was striking: the room would become energized, and a wisdom and openness emerged from these young people that was breathtaking. They were starved for a formal space that allowed them to explore the depth in themselves and the world around them, and these esoteric discussions yielded

---

11 L. Lippman and H. McIntosh, "The demographics of spirituality and religiosity among youth: international and U.S. patterns," *Child Trends* 21 (2010).
L. Bridges and K. Moore, "Religion and spirituality in childhood and adolescence," *Child Trends* (January 2002).

12 R. Kessler, *The Soul of Education: Helping Students Find Connection, Compassion, and Character at School* (Virginia: ASCD, 2000).

sophisticated critical thinking as well as heartfelt anecdotes and ideas that ignited their minds and hearts. Moreover, in counseling, when there were seemingly no answers to the tragedies that many of these young people faced, often it was their own spiritual beliefs and openness that gave them some solace and response to their despair.

The time is ripe for our young adults to participate in an authentic encounter with the transcendent nature of things. The isolation and meaninglessness that many adolescents experience today may be due in part to living in a postmodern culture where technology is the dominating force of the time. While this culture of technology connects information and people in new, spectacular ways, the quality of the connection can be fractured and superficial, and can create an addictive outer-directedness that takes priority over self-discovery. Our culture needs to offer its young people a soulful balance to this paradigm.

In keeping with the progressive course of our time, this curriculum guide is one of the first of its kind to expand the traditional model of social-emotional learning to include not only mindfulness practices but also "spiritual journeying" as an essential part of girl-centered development.

A Note on Inclusivity

While this guidebook is intended for adolescent girls ages twelve to seventeen, by modifying some of the activities, the curriculum can be effective with many different populations, including all gender identities and various age ranges, from preteens to adults. Additionally, many relevant and related topics not included in this guidebook can be incorporated as complementary material to enrich the curriculum, such as reproductive health and sexuality, body image, feminist/womynist theory, and more. I use the pronouns "she" and "her" throughout, as this curriculum is for self-identified females.

I have created this particular curriculum to be as broad as possible in order to reach a large sphere of girls, but I know, from my years of experience working with young women of color and from the LGBTQ community, that there are many additional issues and concerns for girls in those communities that should be addressed. When working with a particular identity group, it is of crucial importance to include supplemental material on the history and issues of identity that exist within that population. Educators on racial-identity development assert that various aspects of racial identity such as oppression, class, and culture become the central features in adolescent development of girls of color, and the ability to observe the social world critically in terms of race and develop a positive racial identity is essential to the development and empowerment of girls of color.[13] Transgender and gender-fluid girls experience specific issues that also require special awareness, and some activities will need inclusive modifications for differently-abled girls. Therefore the themes and discussions in this guide may be slightly modified to address concerns and issues directly related to a particular identity group; in addition, supplemental reading may be added to create a more specific offering. The Additional Resources on page 187 include suggestions for books, articles, and online spaces that are important in creating an inclusive and truly welcoming environment.

A Final Note

The adage "There's nothing new under the sun" speaks to a fundamental truth about the creative process. Several of the activities featured in this guide are modified from common practices that I learned through youth-development work and workshop facilitation. I have yet to find anyone who knows the original creator of some of these processes, so I was not always able to give credit to those sources. I am in no way attempting to claim that this curriculum is entirely original; rather, it is a combination of original and derivative material that forms an aggregate of ideas. Any mistakes or misrepresentations are entirely my own.

....

13 J. Helms, *Black and White Racial Identity: Theory, Research, and Practice* (New York: Greenwood Press, 1990).

B. Tatum, *Assimilation Blues: Black Families in White Communities, Who Succeeds and Why* (New York: Greenwood Press, 1987).

1
GETTING STARTED

The Curriculum

The curriculum presented in this guidebook is designed to be a creative catalyst for girls to examine and express their ideas, purpose, and worth. It is based on my seventeen years of experience working with adolescent girls and supporting their social-emotional learning; it is intended to provide parents, educators, psychotherapists, and any other adults working with adolescent girls a set of social-emotional lessons and activities to aid young women in a meaningful process of self-actualization. In a step-by-step process that engages teenage girls from a deeply creative and exploratory space, the curriculum incorporates writing, media, music, role-playing, and art processes, in addition to a significant focus on group dialogue and interaction.

This guidebook is intended to be used by adults who teach, counsel, or work in some other way supporting adolescent girls, ages twelve to seventeen (e.g. teachers, afterschool program leaders, community center counselors, or parents who wish to create a group with their daughter and her friends). An adult facilitator will create a group of six to twelve participants who can commit to meeting regularly (ideally once a week), ensure the group has a regular meeting space, and use the curriculum to guide the group's work. The curriculum is ideal for groups of six to twelve, but it can easily be used with whole classrooms as well as between a parent and daughter, or in other one-on-one configurations. The guide's emphasis on groups is based on research showing that while boys' process of individuation is often accomplished through their progressive separation and independence from their parents, girls develop *through* their connections with others, particularly with their peer group and a trusted adult who is not their parent.[1] Thus, in most cases, by providing a safe container for a small collective of girls, who will bond and learn together, adult facilitators are creating an ideal platform for girls' development.

Informed by various psychological theories and practices including relational cultural psychology, humanistic psychology, depth psychology, expressive arts, cognitive/behavioral and Gestalt therapies, the curriculum is divided into four themes based on the developmental needs and issues of adolescent girls: 1) Looks Within (self-awareness/self-esteem), 2) Empathetic Attunement (compassion and communication), 3) Necessary Action (social awareness and connection), and 4) Sacred Living (mindfulness and existential exploration).

Looks Within begins by taking inventory of the social influences that impact a girl's experience, especially as it relates to gender expectations and standards of beauty. In this segment, girls are given the opportunity to create, and place themselves in, their *own* definitions of beauty and worth. The chapter explores girls' personal experiences and familial patterns and how these influences impact individual thought paradigms; it then investigates the relationship between thoughts and emotions and offers tools for observation that help girls transform challenging emotional states into more manageable and meaningful experiences.

Empathetic Attunement discusses and illustrates the inherent differences in human perspectives, while creating the opportunity for girls to experience realities outside their own. Through a lens of mutual experience, girls are exposed to communication tools that enhance integrity, openness, and empathy in their interactions with others. Empathetic Attunement also works to break down dichotomies of good and bad, and right and wrong, into a more expansive, nuanced, and multilayered understanding of people and experiences. This serves to empower participants with more complex and creative responses to life circumstances.

Necessary Action exposes and explores a variety of social issues facing girls and women around the world. Girls then take part in a series of activities that challenge them to investigate their ability to facilitate social change in their immediate environments. Finally, participants identify their own personal talents and interests and begin to visualize potential vocations that incorporate creativity and service.

....
1   C. Gilligan, *In a Different Voice*. (Cambridge, MA: Harvard University Press, 1982).

Sacred Living is an exploration of esoteric ideas and practices that connect girls to a metaconception of the world both inside and outside them. Girls learn how to align themselves with their intuition through mindful awareness and meditation, both to ground themselves and to enrich their experience of the world. Participants also investigate existential questions and concepts from a wide variety of interfaith sources and begin to define for themselves what is meaningful in their conception of the sacred.

Life itself, through its experiences and lessons, is truly the most powerful force in transforming adolescents into young adults. This curriculum is an attempt to respond explicitly and proactively to the needs and the capacity of our young girls and to their right to a healthy and meaningful transition into adulthood.

Structure

This guidebook is divided into four developmental sections, based on different themes; each section contains a series of activities. There is an internal logic to the individual topics and the order of the activities, but facilitators are free to utilize and organize them based on their group's needs. There are forty-two lessons; ideally, facilitators will present one lesson per week over a span of nine or ten months. Each activity contains the following components:

Quote and Inspiration Quotes primarily from well-known female artists, activists, and writers, summarizing the general theme of the particular lesson and thoughts about the activity to prompt discussion.

Musical Selection Suggested songs that can be played as participants are entering and leaving the group space. The song's lyrics generally reflect the theme of the lesson, and are performed by an eclectic mix of primarily female artists.

Materials A list of supplies needed to accomplish the activity.

Preparation Activities before the session begins. Some preparations may require the facilitator or participants to do something prior to the next scheduled session, usually a week prior.

0040000040000000000040000040000000400000000400040000040000400000400000400000400400000400000040040000040004000

004000

Instructions Step-by-step instructions to carry out the activity.

Group Discussion Focus on questions that promote reflection and provide a catalyst for processing and integrating experiential activities. The group sits in a circle facing each other.

Facilitators introduce the talking piece (any designated object). Any group member who wishes to speak can request the talking piece by raising her hand. Alternatively, the talking piece can be handed to group members in a clockwise rotation, so that whoever chooses to speak may do so and then pass the talking piece. If a member chooses not to speak, they will continue to pass the talking piece.

Whoever has the talking piece has the invitation to speak. Everyone else is asked to listen intently, without exhibiting judgment, either through words, sound effects, or facial expressions. If group members agree with a statement made by the speaker, they may snap their fingers in agreement. The speaker should speak from their experience, starting their statements with phrases like "I feel," "I believe," or "my experience has been. . . ." Speakers should also be mindful to balance the time they're talking; each girl should have the opportunity to fully express her ideas and experiences and also allow time for others to speak.

It is essential that ground rules (see the Ground Rules section) are established and respected especially during these group discussions.

Parent Path

This section of the lesson plan is specially designed for parents and guardians to implement with their daughters. I use the term "parents" as shorthand to refer to any adults raising girls. I want to acknowledge that these adults are often not parents but aunties, grandparents, family friends, or others who have stepped in and often go unrecognized. Adults working individually with adolescent girls in a different context can also find many of these activities useful. Parent Path activities tend to be more personal in nature but still reflect the general theme of the lesson.

The Facilitator's Role

While the content of this curriculum provides a platform for awareness and growth, a group's rapport, more than anything, will determine the success of the material provided. Group chemistry is often a mysterious affair but is always enhanced by the presence of three basic elements: safety, respect, and openness. These three key ingredients address the participants' ability to set limits of disclosure and ensure the group's ability to maintain confidentiality and to hold every idea with value and respect. Safety, respect, and openness should be incorporated early in the group process by developing behavioral and communication norms (see Getting Started for examples of group ground rules), which group members themselves establish and which they will agree to uphold. The facilitator can aid in this process by consistently monitoring the group's dynamics and his or her own behavior in relation to the ground rules, eventually allowing group members to co-manage their own process.

As an adult facilitator, you bring enormous benefit to the group through your ability to be authentic in the group process. Authenticity can be demonstrated by sharing anecdotes from your own life to illustrate an idea or concept connected to the theme of an activity; in addition, truth-telling or speaking candidly about one's experience or about society in general without sugar-coating reality is key to forming an authentic bond and supportive relationship. Facilitators should be careful not to use these moments of transparency as their own therapy session or philosophical platform, but by modeling this type of authenticity, facilitators are demonstrating that vulnerability can liberate and connect participants. Your real-life examples and honesty bring relevancy and life to the concepts presented, deepen your relationship with the group, and reinvigorate the art of storytelling as an educational tool. In addition, it is crucially important that you are as aware and thoughtful as possible about your own biases, communication style, and inclusivity efforts.

The facilitator's capacity to allow difficult conversations to emerge and evolve, rather than restricting them out of fear or needing to make a point, will also contribute to creating an authentic and safe space. While the guide offers concrete activities, these exist primarily to incite living dialogue. Too many set goals and expectations for a given activity or discussion can restrict its fluidity and organic growth. As a facilitator, you will be asked to use your own intuition and allow ample space for participants to explore moments that feel juicy, or full of depth of perspective or emotion. Conversely, if a dialogue meanders or feels dry, you may choose to acknowledge that point, check in with participants, and then move the conversation to topic that is more energized.

From a mental-health standpoint, this curriculum is based on a preventive model, meaning that it is intended to be used with moderate- and high-functioning populations and contains more structured activities than a traditional therapeutic group. However, because of the nature of some of the themes presented, the activities can, at times, elicit a wide variety of emotions and reactions from participants. Many adults using this guide may not be psychotherapists, and so may not be prepared or even comfortable with the emotional responses that emerge from a group process with adolescent girls. If a moment should occur that activates some emotional response from a participant, it is essential that you hold space for it. This means pausing the group activity or dialogue and allowing enough space and time for the participant to express herself, whether through words or emotions, without the facilitator's or any group members' judgment or need to "fix" the emotional response or the participant. It requires compassionate silence and reflective listening. Safely holding the space requires that everyone involved understands that sadness and anger are important and necessary in the processes of healing; the ability of those in one's environment to be able to protect and respectfully hold the emergence of the authentic self, in all its forms, makes it possible for an individual to undergo an enduring psychological evolution.[2]

....

2   R. Kegan, *The Evolving Self: Problem and Process in Human Development* (Cambridge, MA. Harvard University Press, 1983).

Setting the Tone

As the adult facilitator, it is important, early on, to establish a set of consistent practices used at the beginning of every meeting that create a space of inclusion and safety. These rituals are designed not only to ground participants, set intention, and foster respect and connection; they are markers for participants to know that they are entering a special space. The following are a few suggested opening practices to begin each session that may be incorporated early on.

CREATING INTENTION

At the doorway of the meeting space, each girl sets an intention. This way, before entering the room, participants form a desire for what they want to accomplish during the session. The facilitator may have examples of intentions written out and placed outside the doorway, or girls may formulate their own. In addition, at the closing of each session, participants are invited to identify an intention for the upcoming week. They may vocalize that intention to the group, or you may ask them to write it in their journals. At the end of the next session, they can reflect on their former intentions and create a new one.

Another suggestion involves inviting participants to "cleanse" themselves of negative thoughts and energy by providing burning sage or cedar, or a decorative bowl of water infused with an essential oil like lavender or rose, at the doorway of the meeting space. Participants can cover their bodies with the smoke or sprinkle water on themselves before entering the space and make the intention to release any negativity, entering the session feeling clearer and more present.

MUSIC

Upon entering the space, participants may be greeted with music. The music can be an eclectic mix—jazz, hip-hop, R&B, or rock—and should contain lyrics that are either positive or pertain to the themes that the group will be exploring that day. Songs are provided throughout this guide that reflect the theme of the day, but facilitators may use their own as well.

GREETINGS

Upon entering the room, encourage girls to greet everyone in the room. This may be done with a handshake, fist bump, hug, or secret handshake created by the group.

CHECK-INS

Finally, once all participants are seated, allow for a moment of silent reflection. Invite participants to notice how they are feeling *at that moment*; they may focus on the physical sensations they are experiencing as well as noticing their emotional and mental space. When the designated time has passed for silent reflection, ask participants to share with the group what came up for them, making clear that other participants are not to respond to what is being shared, but are to be fully present and listen. Generally, each participant can be given between one and five minutes to share with the group, depending on how many participants are in the room. The facilitator may sound a bell at the end of the time to let each participant know that she should begin closing her check-in.

Facilitator Contribution

Although it is essential that the participants are the driving contributors throughout the entire process, at the first meeting facilitators can share a bit about themselves, including a few details about their own adolescent experience and why they believe providing a process for girls to learn about themselves, and the world, is important. The purpose here is to set and model, early on, a tone of openness within the group.

Ice Breakers

It is ideal at the beginning of any group formation to create a fun and interactive process that allows group members to slowly get to know one another in a playful and nonthreatening manner. You may take a day or several weeks for this process. A few suggestions for ice breakers are included at the beginning of the next chapter.

Ground Rules

After participants have begun to get to know one another through some initial activities, the facilitator should initiate a process to establish ground rules. Setting ground rules, or norms of communication and behavior, in any group process is strongly recommended. The participants themselves should generate the ground rules through a brainstorming session that can be recorded on a large poster-size paper or board. It is the facilitator's responsibility to make sure that respect, emotional safety, and the intention for openness are included. Once all the suggestions have been recorded, the group, with the facilitator's assistance, can streamline the suggestions by eliminating redundancies and making a concise list.

After this list has been created, the facilitator should initiate a discussion about the guidelines. Participants may be asked what they think of particular rules, why they think the ground rules are important, and what should happen if a participant violates the rules; this kind of questioning allows participants to have a clearer understanding of the boundaries and the meaning of their rules. The following are examples of ground rules that might be included in a group's list:

Confidentiality*

One mic: Allow participants to finish speaking without interruption

I-statements: Beginning any statement of personal belief or
experience with "I feel . . ." or "My experience is . . ."

Openness and honesty

Listening and discovering rather than giving advice

The right to pass

No putdowns or judgments—neither verbal nor through body
language

An intention to be fully present and supportive of other participants

Shared talk space: If you tend to express yourself frequently, be
mindful to pull back at times

---

* **An important note on confidentiality:** Confidentiality should be incorporated into all group ground rules. However, it is essential, from the first session, that facilitators let participants know that confidentiality may be breached in the event that information comes out strongly indicating that a participant is being abused or that there is a danger of suicide. It is important for participants to know why this is the case and to understand that the facilitator will make every effort to collaborate with the participant to find the most respectful way to alert her parents and/or authorities and support her in getting outside help.

PARENT PATH

Parents can regularly incorporate small rituals with their daughters. While your daughter may protest at first, these modest rituals can create a rare and consistent moment where you and she can come together without demands, expectations, and conflict. Below are a few examples of creative rituals generated by parents and guardians I have worked with. Create your own and be consistent.

In the evening before bedtime, Maya lies by her daughter and they talk about anything that is bothering them; afterward, they list three things that they are grateful for.

Right before Clarisa and her daughter Nia leave the house for school or work, they come together and pick an "angel card," which are small cards with qualities or values on them (e.g., friendship, strength, compassion). They place the cards in a special place at the doorway so they are reminded of the card when they come home.

Once a week, Kenny and his daughter Haley pick a hiking trail to explore. During the hike, Kenny commits to not saying anything judgmental, critical, or controlling. Kenny's daughter picks a spot on the trail where they meditate for fifteen minutes. They bring back an object from each of their hikes and put it in a special basket at the entrance to their house.

Once a month, Karin and her daughter Tamara write letters to each other, acknowledging something they observed during the month that the other person did or said that impacted them or that they appreciated. They then hide the notes in places where the other will discover them in time.

2

LOOKS WITHIN

One autumn, a mother and daughter come to my office for a psychotherapy consultation. Both ladies have penetrating eyes that seem to be sizing me up and searching for answers. The mother begins, "My daughter's grades have dropped drastically. She has become more and more withdrawn, she's not very interested in much of anything anymore, but more important, she's not happy. She just carries so much"—at this, the mother looks at me directly for the first time in the session—"doubt." I immediately think of Carol Gilligan, Lyn Mikel Brown, and Mary Pipher's work with girls and how common the narrative through time has been of girl's loss of vibrancy, voice, and sense of self.[1] The mother talks about the social stresses her daughter faces in high school and how her daughter's self-esteem has plummeted. I ask the mother to describe her daughter. The mother looks into the distance, "My daughter is creative and kind, very sensitive." Her voice begins to crack, "I just see her dimming. I don't want who I know her to be to go."

I turn my attention to her daughter, whose face has not changed in expression since she's arrived. She is silent, almost holding her breath, trying to keep herself still and small. I ask her to describe herself. She looks around the room, perhaps searching for her thoughts or trying to find an escape, until she finally finds her way to my gaze. "I don't know." I reflect back, "You once knew, but lately you just feel hollow inside?" She nods her head in affirmation. "I don't really think of myself anymore," she quickly adds. I ask, "What do you think about these days?" Almost immediately, she responds, "I focus on others."

1 Lyn Mikel Brown and Carol Gilligan, *Meeting at the Crossroads* (New York: Ballantine Books, 1992).

Mary Pipher, *Reviving Ophelia: Saving the Selves of Adolescent Girls* (New York: Ballantine Books, 1994).

☾ ✳ ☾

Emerging teenagers tend to look outward in their environment for their sense of self and direction; what they often see outside, however, is a culture fueled by conflicting values and other young people who are also trying to find their way. This predicament is akin to someone drowning in a stormy ocean: grasping for others who are also drowning, and to the sea itself, for their survival, not realizing that a reliable lifeboat is just outside their field of vision. There are many kinds of rescue lifeboats that can and do appear at desperate moments in the teenage travail, but none is more significant or lasting than one's own boat—a boat kept afloat by nothing other than self-awareness.

Self-awareness has long been a human aspiration, throughout different cultural contexts. The ancient Greek philosophers Socrates and Aristotle each spoke of the fundamental importance of self-awareness in their oft-repeated quotes, such as "The unexamined life is not worth living," and "Knowing yourself is the beginning of all wisdom." Lao Tzu wrote, "He who knows others is wise; he who knows himself is enlightened." Ancient Egyptian cultures included the development of self-knowledge as a crucial piece in the esoteric teachings of their Mystery Schools. Psychotherapy is an entire field and practice dedicated to self-awareness and now, in the beginning of the twenty-first century, some educational administrators and policymakers in the United States are beginning to recognize the purpose and worth of promoting the development of self-awareness in young people in mainstream education.

Self-awareness is, in part, the ability to step back and observe one's own thoughts and feelings, as well as the ability to cognitively reframe one's experience to see it in new, more productive ways.[2] Howard Gardner, the professor of education and author of *Multiple Intelligences,* calls this internal skill set "intrapersonal intelligence";[3] with these skills, a girl can survive almost any storm.

Girls with developed self-awareness have a keen sense of themselves. They are often good at knowing what they are feeling without getting too lost in their moods. They can see their circumstances from multiple perspectives and thus are able to create more choices for themselves, both in their attitudes and responses.

....

2   Bonnie Benard, *Resiliency: What We Learned.* (San Francisco: West Ed, 2004), 26.

3   Howard Garner, *Multiple Intelligences* (New York: HarperCollins, 1993), 24–26.

They can identify their own strengths and weaknesses and learn from them. They are able to look inward and access their intuition, which can aid them in wise decision-making. They can search out meaning from their environment, and as a result have a greater sense of grounding in the world.

Looks Within, this first chapter in the curriculum, is dedicated to supporting and expanding girls' intrapersonal development. There are exercises intended to increase girls' sense of themselves and enhance their self-esteem (Beauty Export, Boxed In, and Multiple Personalities). Girls will also participate in a series of powerful exercises that have them identify agents of socialization: how the media and their peers, family, and experiences have influenced how they think and feel about themselves and the world around them (Beauty Import; Family Mosaic, Parts I and II; Lifeline; Mediacracy; and Things People Told Me). Finally, in the last part of the chapter, girls are exposed to activities that invite greater awareness around their thoughts and feelings and how the two inform their response to their environment, thus giving them more agency in their lives (Choices, Emotion Gallery, Feeling Body, Shadow Boxing, and Power Wheel).

ICE BREAKERS

OVERVIEW

Ice breakers are a wonderful way to have participants, who might otherwise be too timid to do so on first meeting, interact with openness and playfulness. There are hundreds of different ice breakers that facilitators can use, to prompt girls to feel more comfortable, learn more about others in the group, and energize the space. The following are a sample selection.

Name Calling

PREPARATION

If the facilitator is working with a relatively small group and can learn participants' names ahead of time, he or she can do a bit of research online to find out the origins and meanings of the names, and then present this information after each participant introduces herself.

INSTRUCTIONS

When a group first meets, I like to talk about the significance of names, and have each girl say her name and one feature about it that she would like to share. For example, what, if anything, does her name mean? Who named her and why did they pick that name? Does she like her name, and if not, what would she choose? Encourage discussion during the exercise. In addition to sharing, have each girl say the name(s) of the girl who shared prior to her. This exercise is a lively way for participants to learn and remember group members' names.

Circle of Friends

PREPARATIONS

Provide a playlist of upbeat music. Clear enough space in the room so that girls can freely move around.

INSTRUCTIONS

✳ When the music begins, encourage the girls to dance, using as much of the room as possible. If participants feel reluctant to dance, they can walk around the room. Every time a group member passes another participant they will give each other a high five. The facilitator will, at random, stop the music, and girls should form into pairs with whoever is closest to them.

   Note: If there are an uneven number of participants, one group can form into a triad. In larger groups, any girls who have not identified a partner should raise their hands so they can locate other members of the group who also do not have a partner.

✳ Once everyone has a partner, ask partners to shake hands and introduce themselves again. The facilitator will then prompt a question (see examples provided below). Partners will take turns responding and listening. Once the facilitator gets the sense that all the pairs have responded to the question, the facilitator will again turn the music on. Participants are encouraged to thank their partner for sharing and move about the room in the same manner as before, dancing or walking and then finding a partner when the music stops. Repeat until pairs have responded to all of the facilitator's questions.

SAMPLE QUESTIONS:

- What is something that people would not know about you at first glance?
- If you had to describe yourself as a river, lake, or ocean, which would it be, and why?
- Describe the things you look for in a friend?
- What is the quality you like most about yourself? What is something you want to improve about yourself?
- If you could have any talent or skill in the world what would it be?

ICE BREAKERS

- If you have a whole day free to yourself, what do you usually end up doing with your time? What would you really want to do with that time?
- Describe something that people do that really makes you angry.
- Who or what do you consider to be your community?
- If you could transform something about your community, what would it be?
- What do you like most about being a girl?
- If you were given one million dollars, what would you do with it?
- How do you think your friends influence how you think or behave?
- What is your racial/ethnic background? Is your background important to you? Why or why not?
- Talk about a place, person, or experience that profoundly changed or inspired you.
- What three things are you most grateful for?
- If you were to die today, what would be the thing you are the most proud of?

Group Discussion

After these two ice breakers, groups generally have broken down some initial barriers and are ready to talk more freely. Have participants form a circle and initiate the discussion with the following questions:

- What was it like sharing? What did you notice about yourself during these ice breakers (e.g., judgments, fears, etc.)?
- What do you think prevents girls from talking openly and honestly to other girls that they don't know?
- Describe what you felt when you first came into the group compared to how you feel now.
- What do you need from others so that you can feel free to be yourself?

ICE BREAKERS

PARENT PATH ....

Creative, in-depth questions, like those used in the sample questions above, are a wonderful way for both children and parents to reveal a deeper, humanized version of their ideas on a variety of subjects not ordinarily discussed. Questions like these can be generated by both parent and daughter, written down on a small piece of paper, and put into a basket. They can be randomly drawn in one sitting as a listening activity, or one can be chosen every night after dinner. The point is to be as honest and open as possible, and to refrain from corrections or criticisms afterward.

ICE BREAKERS

BOXED IN

**"I AM—the two most powerful words,
for what you put after them shapes your reality."**
—UNKNOWN

INSPIRATION

One of the dangers of making initial judgments of people based on their external appearance is that this minimizes and distorts the complexity of who they are. In addition to the more obvious identity categories such as gender, ethnicity, and age, an individual's interests, talents, beliefs, relationships, involvements, and challenges are contributing factors to the rich tapestry of what makes a person uniquely and fully themselves.

MUSICAL SELECTION

Edie Brickell, "What I Am"

MATERIALS

A copy of Personal Profile worksheet for each participant

PREPARATION

Download and print out Bobbie Harro's article "The Cycle of Socialization."[4] Make a copy for all participants and ask them to read it prior to the session.

INSTRUCTIONS

* Begin session by initiating a basic discussion about the Bobbie Harro article. The following are some suggested discussion questions:
  * **Give examples of social identities.**
  * **Give examples of agents of socialization.**
  * **How are we "socialized" into a social identity?**

....

4 Bobbie Harro, "The Cycle of Socialization." (https://canvas.instructure.com/files/33064220/download?...frd...).

- **Describe a dominant identity. What privileges or advantages does being in a dominant group give you? Give examples from your own life.**
- **Describe a target identity. What are the disadvantages of belonging to a target group? Give examples.**
- **Do we come into the world equal? Explain.**
- **What is internalized oppression? Give an example.**

✳ Pass out the Personal Profile worksheet (p. 31) to participants. Have participants fill out the identity boxes at the top of their personal profile.

✳ Have them put a check next to their target identities, and a star next to their dominant identities.

✳ Next, give participants five to ten minutes to write as many identifiers as possible below the line "I am . . .". Have them consider all their involvements, relationships to others, beliefs, interests—encourage them to be creative regarding how they identify themselves and to think outside the box. The facilitator might want to fill out a Personal Profile and use it as an example to illustrate all the different possible characteristics. Examples are provided below:

I am a daughter.

I am a peer counselor.

I am a dancer.

I am a junior.

I am first generation American.

I am intelligent.

I am a dog lover.

I am a Capricorn.

I am a morning person.

I am learning disabled.

I am a sister.

I am an activist.

I am a cisgender, heterosexual female.

I am a New Yorker.

I am a Catholic.

I am a friend.

I am an introvert.

✳ After coming up with as many self-generated identifiers as possible, ask participants to tear or cut on the dotted line of the Personal Profile worksheet, and separate their social identities (how people see them) from their self-generated identifiers (how they see themselves). Then, ask them to lay the self-generated profiles face down in a pile. Each girl can then pick up, at random, a profile with the objective of finding the girl that fits the profile they selected.

Girls will do so by approaching another participant and reading out loud each identifier from the profile. Her partner will state, "I am," if the identifier applies to her, even if the identifier being read is not one that she wrote herself. The exercise will continue until there is an identifier that does not apply, at which point the participant will respond, "I am not." Once both pairs have shared their respective profiles, they may move on to another participant until they find the source of the profile. The activity ends when all girls have been identified with their corresponding profiles. A Group Discussion should follow.

GROUP DISCUSSION

- How many (I am . . .) identifiers did you end up with in your own Personal Profile?
- What characteristics do you think others most identify with you? Which ones do you most identify with yourself?
- Take a look at your whole profile. What could you say about yourself based on the identifiers you see listed? (Ask for volunteers or go around the circle and have each participant respond.)

PARENT PATH

Fill out a Personal Profile with your daughter, identifying as many characteristics for themselves as possible. Next, parent and daughter generate identity characteristics for the other. After these lists have been made, have each person read out loud the identifiers they created for the other. As each identifier is expressed, the other person checks off any that she also wrote on the Personal Profile. Compare which identifiers were checked off and which were not. In addition, discuss similarities and differences in the two profiles.

Personal Profile worksheet

People see . . .

Race

Gender

Age

- -

I am . . .

_____

_____

_____

_____

_____

_____

_____

_____

_____

_____

_____

_____

MULTIPLE PERSONALITIES

> "We do not grow absolutely chronologically. We grow sometimes in one dimension and not in another. We are relative. We are mature in one realm, childish in another . . . We are made of layers, cells, constellations."
>
> —ANAÏS NIN

INSPIRATION

Young people are on a path to find out who they are. However, self-identity is not a singular thing. The self is made up of many different parts; some qualities that are prominent to ourselves and others, and other characteristics are more hidden, because they are less developed or in some cases unwanted. If we are to truly know ourselves, we must come to terms with all aspects of us. All parts have a role to play on many stages and in relation to many different actors.

MUSICAL SELECTION

Regina Spektor, "Man with a Thousand Faces"

MATERIALS

A copy of Multiple Personality worksheet for each participant

INSTRUCTIONS

✳ Discuss with the group how and why different people and environments may bring out different aspects of one's personality.

✳ Have participants fill out a Multiple Personality worksheet.

✳ Follow up with a discussion.

GROUP DISCUSSION

- What qualities do you like most in yourself?
- Which qualities are you embarrassed by or do you dislike?
- Who brings out your best qualities?
- Who brings out your worst qualities?

- What qualities do you look for in a person when you're developing new relationships?
- How do you know when a relationship is not good for you? Give an example from your life, if possible. Are there early warning signs? What do you see? What do you feel? What do you usually do with this information?
- Do you believe you know your truest self?
- How would you describe your truest self?

PARENT PATH

You and your daughter may fill out the Multiple Personality worksheet separately. As a parent, you may replace certain categories, for example: change teacher for boss, and add your children to the list. As an alternative, you can each fill out the worksheet for the other, thus connecting the people listed to the qualities you see come out in your daughter when she's with them. For example, your daughter would fill in column one, and you would connect the people she's listed to the qualities you see emerge in her when she's with them, and vice versa. Afterward, each of you can share and discuss your observations. You can also include the discussion questions from the Group Discussion.

Multiple Personality worksheet

Draw lines from one category to another, and note your comfort level
with each person on a scale of 1 to 5.

Mom

Dad

Sibling _____
NAME

Sibling _____
NAME

Friend #1 _____
NAME

Friend #2 _____
NAME

Friend #3 _____
NAME

Teacher #1 _____
NAME

Teacher #2 _____
NAME

Peer (strangers)

Adult (strangers)

Other _____
NAME

Other _____
NAME

Excited
Wise
Manipulative
Cruel
Judgmental
Jealous
Boisterous
Playful
Generous
Insecure
Flirtatious
Creative
Stubborn
Angry
Moody
Loyal
Sarcastic
Withdrawn
Spacey
Skeptical
Free-Spirited
Shy
Intellectual
Forceful
Passive
Peaceful
Grounded
Proud
Protective
Needy
Careless

THINGS PEOPLE TOLD ME

"No one can make you feel inferior without your consent."
—ELEANOR ROOSEVELT

INSPIRATION

The positive and negative messages girls receive about themselves from others can serve as powerful agents that contribute to how girls imagine themselves in the world. These messages, whether valid or not, are often internalized as "self-talk" and have a profound impact on a girl's self-esteem, reinforcing moment by moment her own mantra of failure or empowerment.

MUSICAL SELECTION

Christina Aguilera, "Beautiful"

MATERIALS

At least twelve sheets of sticky easel paper 25"x30"
Felt-tip pens (one for each participant)

PREPARATION

Place the large easel papers on the wall around the room, and in bold, print on the top of the page the following categories (the facilitator may come up with or add categories of their own):

Academic

Appearance

Body

Emotional Expression

Sexuality

THINGS PEOPLE TOLD ME

INSTRUCTIONS

* Turn on the musical selection and invite all participants to take a pen and randomly circulate around to each of the topics. For each topic featured at the top of the easel paper, participants can write down any disparaging and/ or stereotypical comments or experiences that they have heard, witnessed, or experienced pertaining to their gender. For example, under the topic "Emotional Expression," girls could write: "Catty," "Too sensitive," "People walk out of my life when I am needy."

* In addition, if a participant identifies a comment or experience already written down by another participant that she too has experienced, heard, or witnessed, she may put a check beside the word or phrase. This activity should be done without any talking. Musical accompaniment is encouraged.

* When members of the group have individually finished, they may sit down in silence until all members have finished. Follow up with a discussion.

GROUP DISCUSSION

* Ask volunteers to read aloud, category by category, what participants wrote. Discuss what they see emerging.

* Talk about participants' ideas regarding how negative and stereotypical beliefs regarding females have become perpetuated in their own perceptions and behaviors (you may want to reference the concept of "internalized oppression" in the Harro article introduced in Boxed In).

INSTRUCTIONS, PART II

* Beside each of the original easel papers, place a new sheet of paper with the identical topic written in bold on the top of the page. Invite girls to again circulate around to each topic and write on the new paper their own personal perceptions and experiences that *contradict* some of the stereotypical perceptions of females for each given topic. For example, under the topic "Emotional Expression," girls record: "Fierce," "Vulnerability = Strength," and "I have a hard time

expressing emotion." As before, have girls put a check next to comments that resemble their own beliefs and experiences.

When girls have finished writing, follow up with a group discussion.

GROUP DISCUSSION

Have volunteers read aloud what participants wrote and discuss qualities they see emerging.

- Why do you think the two lists are so different?
- What's at risk if you are authentic and true to yourself?

PARENT PATH

Families can create a board on which all members can record the comments and actions of other family members that have evoked positive and negative effects on them. The activity allows both child *and* parent to be accountable to one another. The board also helps minimize hostile interactions by providing a nonverbal space for allowing family members, through time, to both express and reflect on family interactions. When a negative comment or behavior has been addressed and resolved, either by the parties involved or because the person writing was able to resolve the issue on their own, it can be erased from the board.

MEDIACRACY

"If you are always trying to be normal, you will never know how amazing you can be."
—MAYA ANGELOU

INSPIRATION

The media sends direct and indirect messages that often shape the landscape of our culture. It frequently holds up a mythical ideal, defines beauty and "the good life," and ultimately leaves its public in a state of envy and with feelings of inferiority. This is especially true for girls and women, who are often depicted in a one-dimensional frame of domesticity or as a vain model or slut. However, when we are able to peer behind the veil of this ruse we find a money-hungry system, promoting images of the female that are only hollow depictions of the fullness and complexity of what it is to be a woman.

MUSICAL SELECTION

Beyonce, "Pretty Hurts"

PREPARATION

Various magazines (both male-centered magazines and pop magazines are great
    resources for the activity)
Several sticky easel papers 25"x30"
Glue or tape

INSTRUCTIONS

✳ Have a definition of "stereotype" displayed on an easel paper.

   Stereotype—A widely held, fixed, and oversimplified image or idea of a particular type of person or thing.

✳ Ask the girls to brainstorm various female stereotypes. You may choose to develop a list of female stereotypes in general or you may want to designate a page to female stereotypes from different races and ethnicities. You may also want to reference in your discussion some of the ideas presented in the Bobbie Harro article, including dominant and target identities, and the dominant group's ability to define norms for others: Discuss the following prompts:

   • **What do you see emerging in this list of stereotypes?**
   • **How do you think stereotypes emerge?**
   • **Who or what promotes stereotypes?**
   • **What purpose do stereotypes serve?**

✳ Have girls get into small groups (three to four participants in each group).

✳ Pass out magazines to the small groups and give them from twenty to thirty minutes to find and cut out examples of female stereotypical images or descriptions.

✳ After the time allotted, have participants choose a presenter from the group who will share with the larger group what they have identified. During the presentations, ask someone else from the group tape or glue the images they picked out on a blank easel paper. Each group will post then their images and words on the same easel paper to form a pictorial montage.

✳ Facilitate a discussion at the end of the session about the images and phrases they selected. If there is an absence of images from a particular identity group, make sure that is discussed.

✳ Ask the girls what they want to do with the montage of images and words. A few examples could include: 1) creatively elaborating on the images and making it an art piece, critiquing media images of women; 2) asking girls to develop poems using the montage as a prompt; or 3) having a group rite of destruction.

MEDIACRACY

PARENT PATH

With your daughter, brainstorm as many female gender stereotypes as you can and write them as a list on two separate pieces of paper. Next, spend some time with your daughter surfing through television programs; include commercials, music videos, and popular sitcoms, identifying and checking off on your list as many gender stereotypes as possible. At the end, compare how many checks each of you have, identifying which stereotypes seemed most prevalent.

Follow up every once in a while by dialoguing with your daughter when a particular image or message that exemplifies a gender stereotype is presented in the media. The dialogue does not have to occur every time a stereotype is presented, but just often enough for your daughter to begin to discern and question the images that are being fed to her on a daily basis.

BEAUTY IMPORT

"People often say that beauty is in the eye of the beholder. The most liberating thing about beauty is realizing that you are the beholder."
—SALMA HAYEK

INSPIRATION

A global survey conducted by a Dove ad campaign uncovered that a mere 4 percent of women and 11 percent of girls around the world consider themselves beautiful. The report revealed that while many gains have been made in the last century for women's rights and opportunities, women still struggle with the fundamental issue of self-love and acceptance. Women's ability to embody their own definitions of beauty, rather than what is dictated by others, is a significant step toward the fulfillment of their empowerment.

MUSICAL SELECTION

TLC, "Unpretty"

MATERIALS

Sticky easel board 25"x30"
Computer/video screen connected to the Internet
Camera or camera phone
Pens

PREPARATION

Cue or bookmark selected sites from the Internet so they are ready to go when you present them to participants.

BEAUTY IMPORT

INSTRUCTIONS

✳ Show one or all of the following links to the girls and initiate the corresponding discussion points after each video.

Always, Like a Girl—http://youtu.be/XjJQBjWYDTs

• **Is there any way in which you may or may not be engaging in something because "you're a girl"? What messages did you receive when you were younger about being a girl?**

> More than six out of ten girls ages fifteen to seventeen avoid regular daily activities, such as attending school, trying out for a team sport, or going to the beach, because they feel bad about their looks.[5]

Dove, Beauty Pressure—http://youtu.be/Ei6JvK0W60I

• **What is your initial feeling after viewing this video?**

• **From whom or from where do you get pressure, directly or indirectly, to look a certain way?**

> More than 90 percent of girls ages fifteen to seventeen want to change at least one aspect of their physical appearance, with body weight ranking the highest.[6]

Dove, Evolution—http://youtu.be/iYhCn0jf46U

• **What do you do to improve your looks? How long does it take? Take a moment and write down all your beauty products (hair products, makeup, etc.) and how much they cost. Why do you think advertisers might want to promote beauty standards in such an exaggerated and distorted manner?**

> Eighty-two percent of women feel that beauty standards set by social media are unrealistic; most runway models meet the Body Mass Index criteria for anorexia.[7]

....

5   The Dove Campaign for Real Beauty, www.dove.us/Social-Mission/campaign-for-real-beauty.aspx.

6   Ibid.

7   Ibid.

BEAUTY IMPORT

✳ On a large easel, write the phrase "Beauty is..." and ask the girls what, in their opinion, makes a woman beautiful. Make sure the group talks about internal and external beauty. Record all participant responses on the paper and then post it on a wall or other hard surface.

✳ Have the girls look over the recorded responses pertaining to the prompt. Then have them approach the poster board and put a check next to those qualities that they believe they possess.

✳ At the end of the session, provide free time for the group. Find a space a little away from the group, and call each girl over individually. Ask if you may take a picture of her for an upcoming activity. If you get permission, ask her before taking the picture to close her eyes and feel her beauty, not just focusing on her physical attributes, but drawing forward the qualities of inner beauty that she holds. When she feels she has connected to her beauty, whatever that is for her, have her open her eyes; then you may take a few photos of her. If she does not give you permission, ask if she has a photo of herself that she likes that she could text or email to you before the next group session.

BEAUTY IMPORT

PARENT PATH

Together you and your daughter can make a playlist of empowering songs and play it often in the car or house. Below are examples of some choices, but you can also add any of the songs included in the Musical Selection sections throughout this book.

India Arie, "Strength, Courage, and Wisdom"

Alicia Keys, "A Woman's Worth"

James Bay, "Let It Go"

Sara Bareilles, "Satellite Call"

Maria Mean, "Fragile"

Colbie Caillat, "Try"

Kacey Musgraves, "Follow Your Arrow"

Pink, "Perfect"

Lee Ann Womack, "I Hope You Can Dance"

BEAUTY EXPORT

"We gain our freedom when we learn our true nature."
—TAGORE

INSPIRATION

Beauty is not a prescription; it is a quality that evokes something inside us to pause and open. Beauty carries with it radiance and authenticity; it can be recognized because it resonates with what is within us. We see beauty because we are intrinsically beautiful. When we cut off our ability to see the beauty of others through negative judgments and comparisons, we create a pattern of perception that ultimately shuts us off from seeing and feeling our own radiance.

MUSICAL SELECTION

Cyndi Lauper, "True Colors"

MATERIALS

Post-It notes
A pen for each participant

PREPARATION (prior to actual session)

Download and print a color photo of each girl (gathered from the previous session). Post the pictures in a designated area in the room.

INSTRUCTIONS

✳ Conduct a circle group around the following:

- Have you seen or experienced a lot of competition among girls? What does that look like among your peers?
- When you meet another girl for the first time, do you tend to compare her to yourself, find her faults, or see her beauty and strengths?
- What do you think this kind of comparing does to you?
- What do you think this comparing does to your relationship with other females?
- Do you think when you feel good about yourself, it's easier to see the beauty or the faults in others? Explain.

✳ Pass out Post-It notes to all the girls. Each girl should get at least as many Post-It notes as there are members of the group. For example, if there are ten girls in the group, each girl should get at least ten Post-Its.

✳ Gather the girls around the space where you have placed their photos. Play the musical selection and ask the girls to go to each photo (in no particular order) and write one quality (internal or external) about the girl that makes her beautiful and post it near her photo. Ask each girl to skip her own photo the first time around.

✳ When all the girls have finished writing qualities for others in the group, have them reconvene. The last remaining Post-It is designated for each girl to identify and write a favorite quality about herself that she believes makes her beautiful. Once she has identified and written something on the Post-It, she may approach her own picture, place the note near it, and then read the feedback from other group members.

GROUP DISCUSSION[8]

- **Was it difficult to identify beautiful qualities about others?**
- **Was it more, less, or equally difficult to identify beautiful qualities in yourself?**
- **What feelings and thoughts came up for you when you read the notes from others?**
- **What effect do you think it would have on people to point out their beauty to them?**

PARENT PATH

On a bathroom or bedroom mirror, place a new Post-It every week with an affirmation of your daughter's physical and internal beauty. She may appear annoyed by the practice, but I have personally heard from girls, in retrospect, how much getting those notes meant.

8   The Dove Campaign for Real Beauty, www.dove.us/Social-Mission/campaign-for-real-beauty.aspx

FAMILY MOSAIC, PART I

**"The task of each family is also the task of all humanity.
This is to cherish the living. Remember those who have gone before
and prepare for those who are not yet born."**
—MARGARET MEAD

INSPIRATION

The family unit can be a powerful transmitter of personality, beliefs, and life trajectory. Moreover, our early interrelation patterns with our family can imprint so deeply that they serve as an unconscious template for many personal relationships that follow, often creating a legacy of relationships based on dysfunction and pain. One of the most heroic feats that an individual can accomplish in her lifetime is to put an end to a cycle of dysfunction that has been perpetuated in a family line through generations—one life, healing those who came before and preserving those who lie ahead.

MUSICAL SELECTION

John Mayer, "Daughters"

MATERIALS

Copies for each participant of the sample genogram and symbol guidelines

Blank paper or journals

Colored pencils or pens

Sticky easel pad 25"x 30"

PREPARATION (prior to actual session)

The facilitator should construct a family genogram *before* facilitating the exercise with the group, to be better prepared to help others through the process.

✳ Prepare and display a symbol key for the following (see p. 49) on large easel papers or a board: family map features; relational patterns; added features; and personality characteristics, skills, and talents.

FAMILY MOSAIC, PART 1

FAMILY MOSAIC, PART I

INSTRUCTIONS

✳ The facilitator will explain that the family mosaic is constructed in four parts:
1) The Family Map; 2) Relational Dynamics; 3) Added Features; and 4) Characteristics, Skills, and Talents.

THE FAMILY MAP

The first part of this exercise requires each participant to construct a family tree. The genogram will focus on three generations: The participant and any siblings placed at the bottom of the page, the participant's parents, stepparents or adoptive or foster parents are placed above the children, and finally, grandparents are placed at the top of the page. Other family members should be left out to keep things simple, unless they play a significant role in the participant's life. Have participants use the whole page, and place family members with as much space between them as possible.

Circles represent all female members.

Squares represent male members.

All paternal and maternal partnerships are connected by a bracket (regardless of marital status).

Stepparents are represented by placing a circle or square next to the biological parent they are partnered with and joining the two with a bracket made up of a series of dashes. Adoptive or foster parent(s) are placed parallel with (but not connected to) the biological parents.

All children are indicated by a line connected to and below the brackets of the parents.

RELATIONAL DYNAMICS

When all three generations have been constructed, relational dynamics should be added. Using the other color pencil or pen, have participants identify and draw the line that represents the relationship dynamic between family members. All family members should have a relational line connected to all other family members represented in the genogram. Participants may use more than one line to represent the relational dynamic; however, to minimize visual complexity they may want to choose one line that *best* represents the dynamic.

Sample Family Map

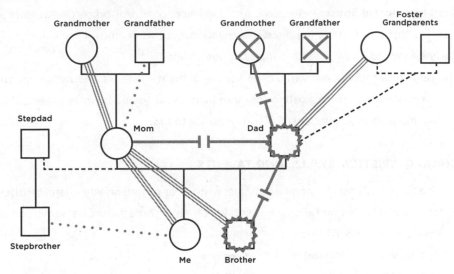

RELATIONAL DYNAMICS KEY

The following lines and symbols represent the relational dynamics participants can incorporate.

Conflictual: A relationship that has significant conflict and tension.

Distant: A relationship in which there is a significant amount of emotional and/or physical distance.

Cut-off: A relationship in which there has been a long period of virtually no contact, perhaps due to abandonment, divorce, or an early death.

Fused: A relationship that is extremely close. May include some elements of conflict and codependency.

Generalized: A relationship that is generally close without elements of codependency.

Drug and alcohol abuse

Early death

Mental illness

ADDED FEATURES

Once relational dynamics are drawn, participants may add other significant features that apply to any of the individual family members. See examples provided.

Drug and alcohol abuse: Individuals who used alcohol and/or drugs (for at least a year) that significantly impaired their relationships, work, and/or behavior.

Early death: Indicates a death before the age of fifty.

Mental illness: Individuals with a clear feature of mental illness (whether or not professionally diagnosed) existing for more than a year (could be intermittent) that has impaired their relationships and/or ability to function.

CHARACTERISTICS, SKILLS, AND TALENTS

✳ Finally, by each family member's name, write a list of personality characteristics, talents, and skills that he or she is known for. Have some examples written on an easel paper or board, such as:

Outgoing	Musical	Sensitive
Peaceful	Athletic	Selfish
Quiet	Ambitious	Thinker
Artistic	Brave	Loving
Talkative	Leader	Free spirit
Needy	Critical	Melancholic

✳ Have participants examine their family mosaic, and then write on blank paper or in their journals what insights into their family and themselves they have gained after analyzing their family genogram. You may suggest the following prompts for participants to write about:

- **What patterns (repeated relational patterns), if any, do you see emerging?**
- **What do you believe to be the source of any familial discord or dysfunction?**
- **What are your families' sources of health, for example, characteristics and accomplishments that are positive protective factors for the family?**
- **What relational dynamics or features do you see in your family that you may be repeating in your relationships outside your family?**

GROUP DISCUSSION

- What was this exercise like for you?
- Are there any insights about your family or your own patterns that you want to share with the group?
- What family pattern would you like to change (or emulate) in your lifetime?

PARENT PATH

This is a particularly good exercise to do with your daughter. Go over the instructions together so that both of you understand how to construct the family genogram. Afterward, each of you can draw *separate* genograms including all the relational dynamics and special features. When you have both finished, share the genograms with each other. Notice what is similar and what is different about the genograms, and begin a dialogue on the discussion questions listed above. This exercise provides a wonderful opportunity to discuss family history, highlight familial patterns, and talk about what has or has not improved with each generation.

FAMILY MOSAIC, PART II

INSTRUCTIONS

✳ Ask for a volunteer from the group who is willing to participate in an exercise about her relationship with her immediate family.

✳ Instruct the volunteer to identify a person from the larger group that will represent her, and find a space in the room where she will be placed.

✳ Next, have the volunteer choose participants from the larger group that will represent members in the volunteer's immediate family (mother, father, stepparents, and siblings).

✳ As the volunteer picks representative members, she will identify each family member and place them in relation to where the participant stands. Thus, the space between a family member and the participant should be demonstrative of the emotional closeness or distance they have with each given family member.

✳ After all family members have been placed in their respective spaces, the volunteer will go to each family member and describe distinctive characteristics or personality traits of that person. For example:

> My father is like a whirlwind; he's fun and always doing something, always working or playing basketball or fixing something. I barely see him sitting down unless it's for dinner. It drives my mother crazy and sometimes it get on my nerves, because he has a hard time listening for more than two minutes.

✳ The designated "family member" will then create a pose that best embodies the volunteer's description.

✳ As an additional option, the volunteer can choose to speak as a "family member" that the facilitator will "interview." The volunteer will stand next to the chosen family member and act as their voice and will respond in the manner and likeness of that family member. The facilitator and the volunteer will then engage in an improvised dialogue using the prompts below:

The facilitator can ask:

• What is your relationship with (name of volunteer)?

• Can you describe (name of the volunteer) to me?

• What is your relationship like with (name of the volunteer)?

- What is something you appreciate about (name of the volunteer)?
- What is something that bothers you about (name of the volunteer)?
- What is one thing that you would like to say to (name of the volunteer) that you have not said before?

GROUP DISCUSSION

- Describe what stood out for you in this exercise?
- Is there any question you would want to ask a family member? Who and what would you ask?
- Describe ways in which you do and do not feel "seen" by the members in your family.
- How much do you think your relationship with your immediate family affects how you feel about yourself and how you relate to others? Explain.

PARENT PATH

A fun and insightful family activity is changing the roles of family members during a family meal. Each family member can choose a different member to portray, or each member can pick names from a hat. Family members will act and perform the roles of their chosen family member, including food preparation, setting the table, and cleaning up. In addition, family members can dress, act, and respond to each other in a way that they believe is representative of the family member they are portraying. After the activity, debrief with the family and have each member talk about what stood out to them about *being* whomever they were depicting. In addition, what stood out while watching someone else portray them?

LIFELINE

"Our life is a path of learning to wake up."
—NATALIE GOLDBERG

INSPIRATION

Our experiences, whether deemed good or bad, are of paramount significance; they form a matrix of memories, with which most of our present and future experiences will be associated. For example, a girl who nearly drowned in the ocean when she was very young may experience the ocean with dread as an adult, perhaps without even knowing why. Our world is often experienced in the context of our past. Some experiences are transient bits of information; others form psychic tattoos that are imprinted for a lifetime. In either case, when our experiences are examined with awareness, we become more mindful of the influence of our responses, and thus we gain agency to change those old patterns of perception.

MUSICAL SELECTION

Alanis Morissette, "You Learn"

During visualization:

Paul Cardall, "Life and Death" (Or any moving instrumental music at least 5 minutes long. Soundtracks often work well.)

After visualization:

Fleetwood Mac, "Landslide"

Melody Gardot, "Some Lessons"

Lalah Hathaway, "Learning to Swim"

Cinematic Orchestra, "To Build a Home"

Shirley Horn, "Here's to Life"

MATERIALS

At least 2 yards of 24"x36" craft paper laid on the floor or a wall.

Two different colors of index cards. Enough for each participant to have ten of
each color.

Pens or pencils

Plenty of tape already cut and ready to go in a designated area

PREPARATION

The facilitator should create a timeline, identifying ages one to eighteen, marking
each year at the top.

INSTRUCTIONS

✳ Discuss the importance of experience and how it can shape an individual's ideas,
identity, and relationship to the world. If possible, use anecdotal examples from
your own life showing how small and big events in your past have shaped who
you are (your beliefs, how you relate to others, etc.) today.

✳ Introduce instructions to participants: Participants will get ten index cards of
two different colors (pass cards out). Place the remainder somewhere accessible

so they can get more if they need them. The facilitator will designate a color for each of the following themes (make sure you have a visual reference for color and theme clearly posted for participants).

Low Points—Major disappointments or challenges in girl's life. For example, "my grandmother got diagnosed with cancer, or my best friend moved to another state."

High Points—Moments of achievement, relationship highs, and moments of pure joy. For example, "getting on the varsity soccer team when I was a sophomore, or going to Mexico on vacation with my family."

✱ Explain to participants that they will write a "title" on each card identifying an event; ask them to get creative with their titles—for example: a first crush may be titled "Love at First Sight." On the backside of the card (lined side), they may write a brief narrative summary about the event.

✱ Let the group know they will participate in a guided-visualization exercise about their life in which they will close their eyes, relax, and just listen to the narration and allow memories to surface throughout the narration. Let the group know that the moments when the facilitator isn't saying anything are there so that they can bring their attention to exploring the images that come up for them without the distraction of the facilitator's voice.

✱ Get participants prepared for the guided visualization. Make sure everyone is comfortable and in a position conducive to turning inward. If possible turn down the lights and try to eliminate outside noise with soft music, without lyrics, that promotes reflection. When reading the narration below, the facilitator should allow silent space for at least thirty seconds to one minute when coming to a pause. Read the following narration in a natural, slow, and calming voice.

> *Close your eyes if you feel comfortable doing so and begin to turn inward. Scan your entire body and notice where you are comfortable and where you are not comfortable and make any needed adjustments. . . . Now allow your body to relax and notice your body's weight drop deeper into the chair or floor. Now bring your attention to the lower part of your body, beginning with your feet. Notice where you may be tensing your muscles and gently relax those muscles.*

(Guide them through various body parts: legs, stomach, chest, shoulders, arms, hands, and face using this same language.)

Now bring your attention to your breath and just notice how you're breathing. You do not need to breathe any certain way; just become aware of your breath. Is it fast or slow? Are you taking deep breaths or shallow breaths? Notice how your body moves with each inhale and exhale **(pause)**. *If you notice that your mind begins to wander to thoughts other than your breath, it's no big deal; just notice that, and gently bring your attention back to your breathing* **(pause)**.

Now imagine that you are standing in front of an elevator door. The doors begin to open and you feel curious about where the elevator would take you, so you walk inside. The elevator door closes and you can feel the elevator rise many stories up. It finally stops and the doors open. As you walk forward, you enter a large, beautiful, old theater with an enormous movie screen. The theater is empty and you take a seat. Suddenly the lights begin to dim, and then your name appears on the screen. What begins to appear is a series of images from your life, beginning with the earliest memories you have of yourself as a child. Moments you vaguely remember, perhaps images from old photographs or vague memories of experiences or feelings from when you were two, three, maybe four years old **(long pause)**.

Now you see yourself beginning kindergarten: your first days of school and how you felt, the first friend you had, your first teacher **(pause)**. *Then images of elementary school begin to emerge: All your teachers from each grade appear, the friends you made. Times you may have been bullied or teased, times you discovered something new, times you felt proud or very happy or alone* **(pause)**. *Your home life also, both big and small moments, both good and challenging times that surrounded your family* **(long pause)**.

Now images of middle school begin to appear. Highs and lows with your friends. New discoveries. Challenges and successes you experienced at school. Times you put yourself in danger. Struggles you were going through with your family. Some lessons you were beginning to learn about people and life in general—all of those moments appear on the screen **(long pause)**.

Finally high school emerges on the screen. These images are clearer, more recent, fun moments with friends, your struggles and accomplishments at school, love, betrayal, your family life **(pause: allow at least one to two minutes).**

The images are slowly now beginning to fade and then these words appear on the screen in bold: YOU ARE MORE THAN THIS. Slowly the screen fades to black. And slowly you begin to orient yourself back to the place and time of the here and now.

✳ Slowly orient the girls back to the present.

✳ Once the visualization is over, allow participants to sit in silence for a moment. Tell participants that when they are ready, they may pick up their color-coded cards and begin to fill them out. Make sure participants are aware of the color of the card and its corresponding category (for example, blue may correspond with "low points" and yellow with "high points"). Make sure participants fill each card with a title of the event. A description on the back is optional but encouraged.

✳ When participants have filled out all the cards, they may begin placing their cards on the timeline (with the tape provided) at the appropriate ages at which the events took place. Cards designated as "high points" can be placed above the line next to the corresponding age. Cards that are "low points" can be placed below the line, next to the corresponding age. Ask participants to sit down in silence when they have completed the task.

> **Note: Ask the girls to remain silent throughout the activity. The music can remain playing, but girls are encouraged to remain focused on their own process and not interact with others. At no point should the girls reveal which cards are their own.**

✳ When everyone has placed their cards on the timeline and is seated, invite the girls to return and look more intimately at the timeline. They may turn cards over to read the narrations on the cards they're curious about. Follow with a discussion.

LIFELINE

GROUP DISCUSSION

- What part of this process stood out to you most?
- What did you learn about yourself through this process?
- What did you learn about others?
- Looking back, do you see anything of value that came from the "low points" of your life?
- Looking at your own "lifeline," would you have changed anything about your life so far? Why or why not?

PARENT PATH

You can do the Lifeline exercise offered here with your daughter and/or with the whole family; however, many girls may not be comfortable revealing certain personal events to their parents, so as an alternative the exercise can be presented as a *family* lifeline. The categories would be slightly altered and related to the family: "High Points"—fun and memorable moments, accomplishments and breakthroughs of the family; "Low Points"—challenging moments, loss, significant conflicts. You may decide to utilize the guided visualization but generally it may be more realistic to go directly into the exercise and for both you and your daughter separately to come up with your own titles and descriptions for each of the categories. After the cards have been filled out and taped down, a dialogue should follow, discussing the following prompts:

What events did we both identify?

Which events were included by one of us and not the other? Why do you think this happened?

Which two or three events (of any of the categories) were most significant for you? Discuss how it affected you and/or the family.

EMOTION GALLERY

"Our feelings are our most genuine paths to knowledge."
—AUDRE LORDE

INSPIRATION

Females are often criticized for feeling and expressing emotions with intensity. Vibrant emotions, however, are nothing to be apologetic about; they are a testimony to our complexity and richness as human beings. Emotions enrich our lives and are a defense against the world becoming sterile. Furthermore, emotions are like audio speakers for our intuition, amplifying our gut reactions to our environment and allowing us to release psychic content that needs to be set free. Our ability to identify, express, and when necessary release our emotions is at the root of self-awareness and is a marker of empowerment.

MUSICAL SELECTION

Joni Mitchell, "Blue"

Nine Inch Nails, "Hurt"

Michael Andrews, "Mad World"

Alanis Morissette, "You Oughta Know"

Nina Simone, "Feeling Good"

Pharrell Williams, "Happy"

MATERIALS

Sticky easel pad 25"x30"

A felt pen for each participant

PREPARATION

On small pieces of paper, write various feeling-states; for example, excited, content, angry, sad, jealous, amorous, embarrassed, or lonely (include as many feeling-states as there are participants). Fold the papers and place into a basket.

INSTRUCTIONS

* Have participants list as many emotions as they can and record them on the easel paper.

* Have participants pick a piece of paper at random from the basket of emotions and reveal which emotion they picked.

* Then ask each girl to think about a physical pose that best portrays the feeling-state they chose.

* Ask each girl to station herself somewhere around the room, with some distance from other participants.

* Give each girl a large easel paper and felt pen. Have them post the paper on a wall or hard surface and write on the top of the page in bold: "I feel (their emotion) when . . ." Below, have them write what triggers that emotion most for them. For example:

  I feel embarrassed when . . .
  I'm asked to do something in front of people and I mess up.

* Have girls get in the pose they created that depicts their feeling-state. They should remain posed until the facilitator releases them (below). Begin playing music (see playlist provided).

* The facilitator will invite one girl at a time to release from her pose and go around to each of the other participants' stations. The facilitator should allow the participant to reach the second or third station before releasing another girl. Participants should circulate stations in order and not at random. At each station participants will write their responses to the prompt on the poster paper. When participants have gone around to all of the stations, they should return to their own station and go back to their pose until the last participant has finished going to all the stations.

EMOTION GALLERY

GROUP DISCUSSION (OR IN DYADS)

- What is your relationship with your emotions? Do you show them often, or almost never?

- Which emotions do you try to hide or avoid?

- Which emotions feel out of your control?

- Which do you feel most often?

- What purpose do emotions serve?

- Can negative emotions elicit anything positive? Give examples.

PARENT PATH

Purchase some balloons of various colors (black, white, red, yellow, blue, etc.). Introduce them to your daughter when she appears stuck in some emotional state. Have her pick the color that best represents her emotion at the time. Have her think of what is bothering her, and have her channel and blow those thoughts into the balloon. Encourage her to focus her thoughts and blow until the balloon is full. Have her tie the balloon and write a word or phrase on the balloon with a felt pen that represents this emotion or an issue she is struggling with. If she's game, invite her to create movement that incorporates the balloon and also is representative of the emotion. For example, perhaps her emotion was angry, so she may slap the balloon across the room several times. Maybe she feels lethargic, so she taps the balloon up in the air and watches it fall to the ground. Finally, tell her that when she is truly ready, she can make a choice to let go of the emotion. She may choose to keep the balloon hanging in her room for a while. However, when she feels it's time, she can take a pin and make an agreement with herself that when she pops the balloon, she will release the emotion. She may then blow up a new balloon, representing a new feeling-state she wants to embrace. Repeat the process.

EMOTION GALLERY

FEELING BODY

**"If you want to know your mind,
your body will always give you a truthful reflection."**
—ECKHART TOLLE

INSPIRATION

We often think of our body and emotions as separate systems, yet when we get stressed, excited, or angry, we feel those emotions in our body; for example, we sweat, or we get butterflies in our stomach, a knot in our neck, or even body tremors. Neuroscientist Candace Pert explains, "Most psychologists treat the mind as disembodied, a phenomenon with little or no connection to the physical body. Conversely, physicians treat the body with no regard to the mind or the emotions. But the body and mind are not separate and we cannot treat one without the other." If our objective is for physical health, we must concurrently strive for emotional equilibrium as well.

MUSICAL SELECTION

Cat Power, "I Feel"

MATERIALS

Five copies of Feeling Body worksheet (page 65) for each participant
Colored markers or crayons

INSTRUCTIONS

* Pass out five copies of the Feeling Body worksheet to each participant and make the colored markers accessible to the group.

* Instruct participants that you will say an emotion and they will turn inward (closing their eyes if they choose); then they will be asked to summon up in their mind an incident that made them feel the given emotion. Ask them to hold the experience in their mind with as much detail as they can. Once they have done this, ask them to reflect on the following:

  Where in their body do they feel this emotion most?

  Is the emotion cool or warm?

Does the emotion have energy and move or is it still and heavy?

If it had a color(s), what would that be?

Is there any image or shape associated with it?

✱ Next, instruct participants to imagine a visual representation of this emotion. For example, it may take form as a kind of black vapor, or whatever color and form they may imagine.

✱ Invite them to release this emotion by first stating to themselves, "This is a feeling; it is not who I am, and now I'm permitting this feeling to leave me." Have participants imagine the image they depicted for the emotion leaving their body and drifting away into the distance.

✱ Participants will open their eyes and, on the worksheet, draw a representation of the emotion that they envisioned; they may draw it on the part of the body where they felt it was sourced or they may draw it leaving their body.

✱ They will repeat this exercise for all five emotions:

Peace, anger, fear, sadness, and joy

GROUP DISCUSSION (Have participants write in their journals and then share)

- What coping mechanisms, both positive and negative, do you use when feeling an emotion that overwhelms you?

- What coping mechanisms have a short-term gain (helping in the immediate moment but having no and often destructive long-term effects)? Which coping mechanisms have a long-term gain (changing over a longer period of time with more lasting effects)?

- On a scale from one to five (five being "almost impossible"), how challenging is it for you to let go of sadness? Stress? Fear? Anger?

- What happens when you begin to look at the emotion objectively (its color, shape, how it feels in the body, etc.)?

- Participants may share their drawings with the group after the exercise.

FEELING BODY

Feeling Body worksheet

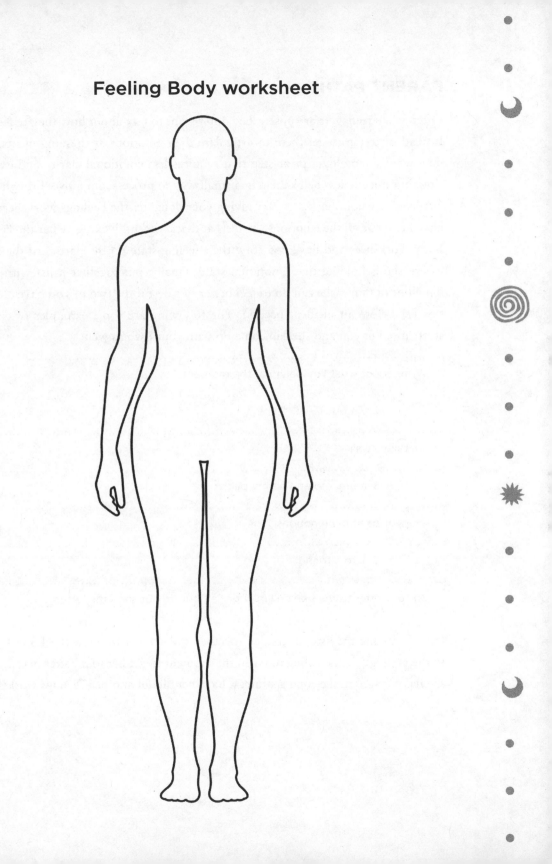

PARENT PATH

Often when teenagers are upset, they don't want to talk about how they're feeling. Instead of trying to get them to articulate their emotions at these moments, you may want to employ a prior step that requires less emotional clarity and expression, but nonetheless helps them in a small way to process and move through their challenging emotional states. Try giving your daughter the Feelings worksheet and have her circle all the emotions she feels at that moment. Next, give her the Feeling Body worksheet and have her draw their feeling-state on the part(s) of the body where she is holding that emotional state. Finally, put together a list with your daughter of things she can do to feel better (it's best if the two of you have created this list before an incident occurs). The following are some examples of coping strategies, but you and she can come up with your own as well:

Write about what I'm feeling at the moment.

Cry it out.

Go take a walk.

Scream into and hit my pillow.

Draw or paint my emotions.

Talk to a friend.

Write a letter to the person I'm angry at, but do not send the letter.

Show her the list you created together and ask her to put a check mark next to the strategy she is willing to try in the moment to get her to a better place. After she has engaged in the coping strategy, have her fill out another Feelings worksheet.

FEELING BODY

Feelings worksheet

| surprised | suspicious | hysterical | guilty | exhausted | disgusted |

| enraged | ashamed | cautious | smug | stressed | angry |

| shy | shocked | anxious | jealous | lonely | sad |

| hopeful | depressed | mischievous | frightened | lovestruck | embarrassed |

| happy | ecstatic | frustrated | content | bored | confident |

Illustration by Nina Soberanis, age 15.

SHADOW-BOXING

"Nothing ever goes away until it has taught us what we need to know."
—PEMA CHÖDRÖN

INSPIRATION

In the unconscious recesses of our psyche, there lies a place where memories, experiences, and beliefs too painful to face are pushed aside and hidden from our conscious self. Like the physical laws governing matter, these psychic imprints do not disappear but rather gather, and can develop into a negative psychic force that manifests in a myriad of ways (for example, depression, excessive worry, internal self-criticism, inexplicable bouts of rage or sadness, and even physical illness). Different sources through time have recognized this destructive psychic energy and labeled it many things: "negative complex,"[9] "pain body"[10] and "wound field,"[11] among others. All of these terms identify a psychic phenomenon sourced in our personal and collective wounds that can wreak havoc with our self-worth, relationships, and general development and success.

Carl Jung said, "To confront a person with [their] own Shadow is to show them their own light." This wisdom can be applied here: it is only through knowing our own shadow—the parts of ourselves that are unwanted and unclaimed—that we can ever truly know and be in full command of our wholeness.

MUSICAL SELECTION

Fiona Apple, "Shadow-Boxing"

MATERIALS

Wide variety of colored pencils and/or markers
Journals

....

9   "About Complexes" (https://analyticalpsychology.wordpress.com/tag/jung/).
10 Eckhart Tolle, *The Power of Now: A Guide to Spiritual Enlightenment* (Vancouver B.C. Namaste Publishing, 1999; Novato, CA: New World Library 2004) 33–42.
11 Mario Martinez, *The Mind Body Code: How to Change the Beliefs that Limit Your Health, Longevity and Success*, (Boulder: Sounds True 2014) 21-44.

INSTRUCTIONS

＊ Introduce the concept presented in the above overview to the group. Make sure you include an example from real life that you can draw on—your own, or one of the samples below. The examples provided are rudimentary scenarios that illustrate how a "shadow wound" (a term I will use repeatedly here), might show up. Be sure to note that these are very involved patterns that manifest in infinite ways and are unique to each individual.

Iana grew up in a community with a lot of violence and poverty. At age seven she lost her father to liver disease due to his drinking problem. Iana was raised by her mother, who loved her very much but was often working so that she could provide for the two of them; they moved four times by the time Iana was twelve. When she was eleven, she started to become very anxious. Every time she entered a room she would create an escape plan "just in case something happened." Iana became so anxious she could hardly do her homework, especially when she was alone, and her grades dropped considerably.

Steph grew up in a two-parent home, in a wealthy part of town. Her parents, both lawyers, were very educated, ambitious perfectionists. They showed Steph love primarily through providing for her physical needs and by setting high expectations. There was very little emotional or physical nurturing in her home but her parents always let her know they were proud when she accomplished something great. Steph got almost all A's in school, participated in the soccer team, played the clarinet, and was in all honors classes. At age fifteen, however, she developed a chronic pain at the base of her back. It became so painful and debilitating that it stopped her from playing soccer and was affecting her grades. Her parents took her to many doctors but none could figure out what was wrong.

Marsha's father and mother divorced when she was nine years old, and she didn't see her father much after that. Marsha's mother was bitter after the divorce and often berated Marsha's father, until a year later when Marsha's mother began a new relationship with another man who became her main focus. When Marsha was seventeen, she ended a two-year relationship that had been verbally and emotionally abusive. She showed very little emotion during or after the breakup and declared she was "over it." She then proceeded to get drunk every weekend and finally was arrested for reckless behavior; she also began a series of sexual relationships and got into frequent fights with her female friends.

SHADOW-BOXING

✳ Ask the girls to reflect for a few moments on their own shadow wound. Remind participants that a shadow wound may manifest in many different ways: through amplified emotions that don't seem to fit the present circumstances, or through recurring health issues and self-sabotaging behaviors that impair relationships, schoolwork, and special opportunities. Have the girls first write in their journals to explore how their shadow wound shows up in their life; ask them to detail the thoughts and feelings that they experience when in the grips of their shadow wound, and what consequences (for example, loss of self-esteem, unhealthy relationships, missed opportunities, or poor grades) they have experienced as a result.

✳ After the free-write, have participants get comfortable and, if possible, turn down the lights. You will guide them through the following visualization. Allow some time between each of the following prompts:

Invite participants to close their eyes and focus on their breath; with each breath ask participants to imagine that they are going internally deeper into themselves.

Ask participants to invite their shadow wound to reveal itself; it may reveal itself as a creature or person, through color and shapes, or in a feeling tone or voice. Remind them to stay open and not judge what may or may not appear (allow a minute or two).

Tell participants to ask whatever comes forward if there is anything it wants them to know. Encourage participants to stay open and curious (allow a couple of minutes).

Finally, remind participants that while what is being revealed is a part of them, it is not the core essence of who they are. It is a part of them that was wounded and then pushed aside. Have participants thank the shadow wound for revealing itself; if they choose, they may send the shadow wound loving compassion. Most important, have participants bring their awareness to the fact that they are *not* their shadow wound, and it is they who can, at any time, decide to take back their power.

Have participants slowly open their eyes and sit for a moment in silence. When they are ready they may get the color pencils/markers and a piece of paper (or they may use their journal) and have them draw, to the best of their ability, what was revealed to them in the visualization. While they are drawing, ask them to think of a name for what came forward during the visualization, and have them label the image once the drawing is complete.

SHADOW-BOXING

GROUP DISCUSSION

✳ The facilitator can ask for volunteers to share any part of the activity: free-write, drawing, or guided visualization experience. Make sure the group is focused on and respectful to whoever is sharing.

✳ For those who are hesitant to share, you may want to ask a more general question about how the exercise was for them.

PARENT PATH

Adolescent girls often experience a great deal of rage that seems out of proportion to their family members, who feel powerless in its wake. If possible, make a hidden video recording of a moment like this. On another day when your daughter is calm and has distanced herself from that experience, show her the video. Ask with genuine, nonjudgmental curiosity about her thoughts after observing herself. Ask what she remembers feeling in that moment and what she thinks she needed. Tell her how you feel when you see her in that state. Be loving and honest. Delete the video in front of her so she knows it won't be shared with others. Witnessing their own behavior can often have a powerful effect on teenagers. After watching their behavior, teenagers can gain some much-needed awareness during future moments when they find themselves in this state of amplification.

POWER CIRCLE

"Your emotions are slaves to your thoughts,
and you are the slave to your emotions."
—ELIZABETH GILBERT

INSPIRATION

Our thoughts are powerful forces that shape our conscious experience. Sourced from past associations and socialization, our thoughts assign meaning to every person, place, and experience we encounter. Moreover, thoughts have an intrinsic relationship to emotions. Our emotions are, in effect, psychic fuel that can propel a simple thought into a highly charged intrapsychic experience that inevitably sparks some form of action in the outer world. Through this understanding of our thoughts we become creators of our own experience. Through conscious awareness, we can observe what interpretations of reality our thoughts are presenting, and then decide for ourselves if that is the path we want to fuel with our feelings and actions.

MUSICAL SELECTION

Aretha Franklin, "Think"

MATERIALS

Sticky easel paper and felt pen

Each participant should receive two copies of the Power Circle worksheet.
   (page 74).

PREPARATION

If possible, view the film *What the #$*! Do We Know*, chapters nine through thirteen, for a good visual breakdown of the relationship between thoughts and emotions. Make sure you review the following concepts after viewing the segment.

   Associative memory

   Long-term thought patterns—"Nerve centers that fire together, wire together."

   Emotional addiction and how an individual can create situations to reinforce their own emotional/chemical need

INSTRUCTIONS

✳ Draw a Power Circle on a piece of easel paper, with its three parts labeled action, thought, and emotion. Talk about the relationship between these elements.

✳ Begin by sharing a personal experience that illustrates how your thoughts (interpretations) and feelings affected an outcome to a situation. It is useful to use examples of a positive thought cycle and a negative thought cycle. Talk about the outcome of each and how your actions might have affected others and their possible interpretation, feelings, and actions in response to yours. Talk about how this entire process is circular—that negativity often begets more negativity. Facilitate an in-depth discussion around the following questions:

- **Does what we've experienced and learned in the past influence how we perceive and interpret things in the present? Explain.**

- **Is it possible that what we are interpreting (thoughts) may be distorted? What effect would that have on the emotions and actions that follow these thoughts?**

- **At what point in this cycle does an individual have power to choose what to do next?**

- **How would one go about rerouting a negative cycle?**

- **What would be most challenging in doing so?**

✳ Next have participants reflect on a situation or event that they experienced negatively. Have them fill out the first Power Circle worksheet, dissecting the four components of the circle: 1) the activating event (words or actions that triggered some type of response); 2) their own thoughts or interpretations of the "activating event"; 3) the feelings that were evoked through the meaning (thoughts) they gave to the activating event; and 4) their action(s) in response to their thoughts, interpretations, and feelings.

✳ After the participants have filled out the first worksheet, have them fill out a new one. On this new worksheet, they will be asked to come up with a secondary interpretation of the original activating event. The new interpretation may include reconsidering someone's intentions or perhaps understanding the event as an important lesson about oneself. Alongside the new interpretation, participants will imagine the consequential feelings, actions, and outcome of this new cycle.

POWER CIRCLE

Power Circle worksheet

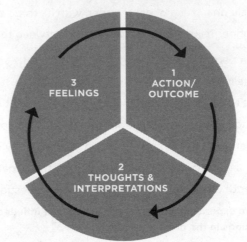

Activating Event: the initial event (words or actions) that triggered your response

_____

_____

Thoughts & Interpretations: your interpretation of the how, what, and why of others' actions

_____

_____

Feelings: the emotions that arose for you based on your interpretation of others' actions

_____

_____

Outcome: your response, based on your thoughts and feelings; the final outcome

_____

_____

✳ **Variation:** Rather than reconstructing new interpretations on their worksheet, participants can share their initial Power Circle worksheet in small groups. Make sure that each participant explains her interpretations and feelings throughout the cycle. The group can then collaboratively brainstorm several new ways of interpreting the activating event that might shift the feelings and outcome of the cycle.

GROUP DISCUSSION

- Do you think you may be "addicted" to a particular emotion? Explain.
- How are these related to one another? Thought = Habit = Reality
- What does it mean to "create your own reality"? Do you believe this is true? Why or why not?

POWER CIRCLE

PARENT PATH

The movie *Inside Out* illustrates in a very basic and entertaining way the relationship between thoughts and feelings. You may want to view the movie together and discuss some of the concepts presented in the film; for example:

> Who are the main characters (feelings) in your brain? You may even want to draw out each of your characters and give them names.

> Which character is most running your show?

> Pick an event or experience and break down how each of the characters would interpret the event.

> Which character would you want to give more power to?

> You may also incorporate into the conversation the following story, an elaboration of a tale frequently attributed to the Cherokee people.

There was a little girl who heard her grandfather in his garage, cursing and slamming cupboards and drawers. When she entered, he realized what he was doing and began to calm himself down. The little girl asked her grandfather, "What's wrong, Grandfather?" The grandfather looked in his granddaughter's eyes and said solemnly, "I have two wolves inside of me, fighting. One wolf is angry, violent, greedy, and cruel. The other wolf is loving, generous, compassionate, honest, and kind. The little girl asked her grandfather with great concern, "Which one will win?" The grandfather responded, "The one that I feed."

POWER CIRCLE

CHOICES

"Being oppressed means the absence of choices."

—bell hooks

INSPIRATION

The power of choice is, among other things, the ability to consciously decide how one will react to a given situation. Our choices, moreover, are not expressed in our actions alone; choice extends to our thoughts as well. We have the opportunity at any given moment to deepen our understanding of a person, place, or event through an array of perspectives, and to choose which thought, action, and reality serve our highest good.

MUSICAL SELECTION

Lauryn Hill, "The Miseducation of Lauryn Hill"

MATERIALS

Sticky easel board 25"x 30"

PREPARATION

Create a space in the room to conduct roleplays.

Post the following scenarios on the easel paper or board.

- A girl leaves her seat for a moment to get something, and when she comes back another girl is sitting there and doesn't want to move.
- A daughter asks her mother if she can go out with her friends Saturday night to an event that is very important to her, and the mother says no.
- A girl walks by a boy who starts verbally harassing her.
- A girl notices a student in her class bullying another student.

Or, girls may use their own scenarios from the Power Circle activity.

INSTRUCTIONS

✳ Ask for volunteer actors who will choose and perform an improvisational scene from one of the scenarios above.

✳ When the scene has progressed to some outcome, the facilitator will freeze the scene and review the action, discussing with the group the various thoughts and feelings the actors might have felt during the exchange.

✳ A new scene with new actors may follow;

Or

✳ One scene may be played out several times with *different* responses from the same actors;

Or

✳ Circulate in new actors, who will have different responses than the preceding actors.

✳ Be clear with participants that there is not necessarily a *right* response, only different and creative responses. Always follow up with a review at the end of the scene of the group's impressions of the possible thoughts and feelings of the characters being portrayed.

GROUP DISCUSSION

- **Give an example of a time in your life when a choice you made had a significant impact.**
- **What do you think may sometimes inhibit your ability to make wise and conscious choices?**
- **What could you do to enhance your decision-making power?**
- **What are some of the benefits and challenges that come with freedom of choice?**

CHOICES

PARENT PATH ....

In moments when you can anticipate your daughter might have an automatic negative reaction to something done or said at home, stop the action and identify
some of the choices (thoughts and actions) that she has, as well as their possible
outcomes. Allow her to choose. Your daughter may not pick the "right" decision,
but by slowing down the process and making it more conscious, you are modeling
more awareness around her decision-making. Try to avoid either-or choices, and
promote creative and multiple options whenever possible. For example:

> *I can see you're angry and frustrated at me for not allowing you to (. . .). You
> might run up to your room and not speak to me for a couple of days, and you
> certainly can do that, but you won't get any of your needs met and we'll be in
> a fight. You also can decide to stay here, and if we can calm down, we'll talk
> through this and maybe we'll be able to work out some kind of compromise.
> You might not get to do exactly what you want, but perhaps more than if you
> left, and we both will feel better than we do right now. We could also forget
> this whole argument and go finger-paint the bathroom door together [or
> something distracting like that]. It's your choice. I'm choosing to stay here and
> work this out with you. I'd like if you stayed too, but I can't choose for you.
> What choice do you want to make that reflects your best self?*

3

EMPATHETIC ATTUNEMENT

In 2001, I was hired by a public high school in Oakland, California, to design and run a conflict-mediation program, led by the students themselves, to help reduce violence at the school. The high school had a population of 1,300 students and was once dubbed "Killer High" in the '90s. The name and the school's reputation for violence, however, had not been entirely lost. I wasn't interested in putting on a dog-and-pony show, introducing a conflict-mediation program that proved the school was trying to do something about the violence but did nothing to truly address it. It was vitally important to me that the program I developed actually worked and that I gave the mediators some concrete skills, because the conflicts that existed at this school were real; they could be vicious and often expanded to include family members from the outside community if they weren't dealt with immediately and effectively.

The program was a success and, by the third year, had significantly reduced the number of physical altercations and thus suspensions at the high school. At the end of one school year, when students tended to become especially restless and agitated, I got a call from a teacher. Two girls had almost gotten into a physical fight; the teacher, fortunately, interrupted the altercation just in time, and because of his relationship with the students, was able to deescalate the confrontation and convince them both to go to a mediation session.

In the mediation room, the girls, Angie and Tatiana, sat across a table from each other. Angie wore all pink and red, and she had a Hello Kitty backpack. Tatiana sported jeans and a t-shirt that said Girls Rule. In contrast to their appearance, their energy was hard and impenetrable, and they both seemed just words away from getting up and launching themselves at each other. I brought in one of my strongest student mediators to talk to the girls, and I observed the session to make sure it remained contained. After the two girls reluctantly agreed to the ground rules, the mediator asked Angie to begin by telling her side of the story. Angie began in a hostile tone. "I was just sitting there and Tatiana comes into the classroom, mean-mugging me for no reason, and then slams her backpack down right near by desk and doesn't say a word. I asked her what was up with her, and she turned around and said, 'None of your —— business.' I'm not going to let anyone talk to me like that. So I said something to her and we got up to fight."

The mediator took a deep breath and employed active listening: "So what I hear you saying is that you believe that Tatiana was mad at you by the look she gave you when she entered the class and slammed her books down." "Yep," Angie responded assuredly. The mediator continued carefully, "So you checked in with Tatiana to see what was wrong but she still was shutting you down and then you felt she disrespected you. You didn't do anything to her that you knew of, so you felt like you didn't deserve that and you needed to let her know she couldn't talk to her like that." "Yep," Angie repeated.

The mediator turned to Tatiana so she could tell her side of the story. Tatiana began in an equally defensive tone. "I came into the room, sat down, and Angie was all like, 'What the —— is wrong with you?' I couldn't deal with anyone's crap today, and so I went off on her." The mediator reflected back, "So from your point of view, you had just entered the room, not mad at Angie or meaning to snap at her, so you were surprised when she asked you, in the way she did, what was happening with you." Tatiana interrupted the mediator, irritated: "Yeah, I just couldn't deal with anyone's BS today." The mediator, skillfully listening, picked up on something, and asked Tatiana a question that changed everything: "I heard you say something about today. 'I couldn't deal with anyone's crap today.' What is it about this day that is so different—that makes it hard to deal with anyone or anything?" There was a long, drawn-out silence, and in the midst of it Tatiana sat in her chair, almost shaking, struggling to keep her stone wall erected. We all sat there patiently, holding space for what might emerge out of her. I then gently said, "We're here with you."

Tatiana's tears began to flow down her face. Her pain was so tangible and tender I believe everyone in that room could feel it. In the course of the session,

Tatiana told us that one year ago, to the day, her brother had been killed in a drive-by shooting. Through her tears she talked about how close she was to him, how much she missed him, and how angry she was that she didn't get to live this life with him in it. When the session finally concluded, the two girls did not make any agreements, shake hands, or make any formal apologies to one another. They didn't have to. There was something far more powerful communicated between the two disputants: a shared, unspoken understanding that life hurts, and that vulnerability and empathy is medicine for that kind of pain.

☾ ☀ ☾

Empathy is the ability to tune in to and understand another's perspectives and feelings. According to Daniel Goleman, author of the highly acclaimed book *Emotional Intelligence*, empathy is one of the central features of emotional intelligence and is comprised of three different variants: 1) *cognitive empathy*, a natural curiosity about other people's reality and the ability to understand another person's perspective and how they think; 2) *emotional empathy*, the ability to intuit another person's feelings through an actual visceral sense; and 3) *empathetic concern*, a genuine call to action on someone else's behalf—it is, in essence, compassion in action.[1] With this more developed definition, it is clear how the characteristics of empathy not only help in relationship development and conflict resolution, but also in the formation of morality, compassion, and resilience in young people.[2]

However, empathy is complex for adolescents, and for girls in particular. Research reveals that there exists a kind of "crisis of connection" for adolescent girls. On one hand, adolescent girls are developmentally primed to look outward to others to inform them about their identity, behavior, and value. Moreover, females are socialized and rewarded for being caring and to think of others, yet this completely outward orientation prompts girls to abandon their *own* ideas, values, and sense of self.[3] Thus girls and young women in Western culture face the challenge

1 Daniel Goleman, *Emotional Intelligence* (New York: Bantam, 2005).
   "Three Kinds of Empathy," uploaded January 26, 2011, www.youtube.com/
   watch?v=eg2pq4Mjeyo
2 Benard, *Resilience*, 15–16.
3 Brown, Gilligan, *Meeting at the Crossroads.*
   Pipher, *Reviving Ophelia.*

of finding their own voice and identity amidst their need to empathize and connect with others.

Empathetic Attunement begins by addressing these intersecting needs of autonomy and connection by allowing safe spaces to express differences of experience and perspective (Boundary Check, Cross the Line, Fish Bowl, Multiple Personalities, and Seeing Double), while giving participants the opportunity to put themselves in another person's reality and expand their empathetic awareness (Herstory, Media Roundtable, and We Clique). Finally, girls will learn tools that will help them navigate conflict with others in a manner that is reflective, and honest, and allows them to voice their own truth and needs (Gold Digger, In Defense of Vulnerability, and Mirror Mirror).

CROSS THE LINE

"It's a terrible thing
To be so open: it is as if my heart
Put on a face and walked into the world . . ."
—SYLVIA PLATH

INSPIRATION

Empathy reminds us that we are not alone. By sharing our inner world with another we create intimacy and alleviate isolation. We also discover that the feelings, thoughts, and experiences we hold as painful, even shameful, are not so uncommon; and that those same experiences can someday serve as a source of validation and encouragement for another who may be challenged with a similar issue.

MUSICAL SELECTION

Ingrid Michaelson, "Everyone"

INSTRUCTIONS

✳ Create two lines on the floor about three yards apart from one another. They may be marked lines or they may just be intended lines. One line will represent "Completely Agree." The other line will represent its opposite, "Totally Disagree." The space in between are shades of the two opposing opinions.

✳ Designate a line that all of the participants will stand on, facing toward the other line. This will be the designated "home base."

✳ The facilitator will read out loud a prompt and the students will silently move to the space between or on the lines that best reflects how they feel about the statement.

✳ Once participants have settled in their respective spaces, they may look around for a moment and then silently return to home base and wait for the next prompt. As an alternative for smaller groups, the facilitator may ask if anyone wishes to elaborate on her thoughts and feelings regarding the prompt. Participants may choose to respond by raising their hands.

✷ Let participants know that the content of the prompts can be very personal and sensitive in nature. Remind participants to be especially mindful of maintaining a safe, nonjudgmental space. Discuss with participants what that looks like before beginning the activity. For example, participants should not make any comments, sounds, or facial expressions in response to how a person identifies themselves by way of the line.

Sample Statements: The facilitator may use some or all of the statements provided or come up with her own.

I am an artist.

I am an athlete.

I am an intellectual.

I am an activist.

I feel different from my peers.

I like school.

I do well academically at school.

I feel stressed because of my school work.

I feel stressed because of my social life at school.

I feel stressed because of my parents.

I have friends I can trust.

I have friends outside my race or ethnic group.

I like being home.

My biological parents live together.

I feel close to my mother.

I feel close to my father.

I feel my parents are too hard on me.

I feel my parents work too much.

Someone in my family struggles with a mental illness.

Someone in my family struggles with drugs or alcohol.

I struggle with depression.

I struggle with anxiety.

I am happy with my body.

At least one of my parents is from another country.

I consider myself nonwhite.

I am proud of my race or ethnicity.

I consider myself to be a part of the LGBTQ community.

I consider myself nonbinary or gender-neutral.

I have been in love.

I have been in an emotionally or physically abusive relationship.

I believe in my ability to love another.

I believe in others' ability to love me.

I consider myself beautiful.

I want to change something about my appearance.

I want to change something about my body.

I like who I am as a person.

I feel confident about my future.

GROUP DISCUSSION

- What was this exercise like for you? What was challenging about it? What was inspiring?

- Did anyone experience being alone on a line? What did that feel like?

- What makes it so hard to be "different"? What is positive about it?

- What has been your experience when you express differences of opinion or identity around your peers?

- What can we do to ally with others when they express differences of opinion or identity?

CROSS THE LINE

WE CLIQUE

**"Contempt is the weapon of the weak and a defense against
one's own despised and unwanted feelings."**
—ALICE MILLER

INSPIRATION

What would it be like to live in the shoes of another? To touch the complexity of another's experience that we have perceived as so one-dimensional? While we may never know the entire field of another person's reality, empathy allows us to extend our awareness to another; showing us that regardless of how different we may look, act, and even think, there is a collective experience of being human that binds us and allows us to escape the limited encasing of the self into greater awareness and compassion for another.

MUSIC SELECTION

KT Tunstall, "(Still A) Weirdo"

MATERIALS

Name labels with adhesive backing (enough for all participants)
Lined paper and tape (one for each participant)
Felt pens for all participants
Journals
Easel pad 25"x30"

INSTRUCTIONS

⋆ Brainstorm with participants about different social cliques at their schools. Record the types on the easel sheet. Have one volunteer also record each type on small pieces of paper and make sure the papers are folded in half. Come up with at least as many identity types as there are participants. Examples of types: "Hipster," "Popular," "Emo," etc. Each group of girls may have their own unique names for these cliques. Have them describe each type as they're being recorded.

* Collect the small pieces of paper and place them in a container. Have each girl pick one at random.

* Have participants write in their journals about a girl from the clique they selected. The girl can be based on someone they know or can be made up; in either case, the participant should come up with an alias for this girl. Participants should write in the form of a first-person narrative. Encourage girls to include one or all of the following points:

  How others perceive me

  What about this stereotype is true of me, and what is not

  What I want people to know about me that they might not see upon first meeting me

* After the girls have written their narratives, have them take an adhesive label and write their social identity on the label and stick it somewhere on the front of their body where others can clearly see it. With the assistance of another group member, they should also tape a piece of lined paper on their back. Everyone should have a felt pen in hand.

* Tell the girls that they will participate in a "mixer." As each girl approaches another in the mixer, she may have a brief conversation if she chooses. Whether she chooses to engage in a conversation or not, she will write on the piece of paper located on the other girl's back, perceptions they have about that particular clique or identity. Everyone should get a chance to write on every girl's back.

* Play some music and begin the mixer. Allow at least fifteen minutes for girls to circulate amongst each other.

* After the allotted time, gather the girls and ask them to take out their narratives. Have each girl read her journal narrative out loud to the group and then remove the paper from her back and read the comments out loud. Follow with a discussion.

WE CLIQUE

GROUP DISCUSSION

- What was your initial feeling when you picked the clique you selected?
- What was it like writing about the experience of someone else? What did you have to do to imagine another's reality?
- Do you think it's possible to completely know another person's reality? Why or why not?
- What was your experience during the mixer?
- Did you feel different about any of the identities after hearing their narratives?
- How was this activity similar to real life experiences you have had around cliques?
- What would motivate you to befriend others who are different from you?

PARENT PATH

Sometimes teenagers and their parents struggle because parents are unwilling to let go of their old perceptions of their children and allow a more evolved version to replace it. Parents can fixate on ideas about their children that are stifling to their emergence into young adulthood. Ask your daughter to write a list of things you say or do as a parent that make her feel that you have pigeonholed her in some way. This information can be used for your own reflection and perhaps to take inventory of any static perceptions you have of your daughter. In addition, you may want to begin acknowledging ways in which you see your daughter growing up: for example, greater responsibilities she's taken on, or growing insight, integrity, and capacity to love others. These acknowledgments may be presented periodically to her in cards she discovers in her room or backpack, or you can make time to just tell her in person when you and she can both be fully present to give and receive that acknowledgment.

WE CLIQUE

SEEING DOUBLE

> **"The enchanting and sometimes terrifying thing is that
> the world can be so many different things to so many different souls.
> That it can be, and is, all of this at the same time."**
> —HENRY MILLER

INSPIRATION

Quantum physics has revealed to us that, among many things, the universe is made up of probabilities and that the observer has a profound effect on what probability will come into existence as reality. In other words, a perception of a person, place, action, or statement can be interpreted in different ways by a multitude of observers. Each observer places her own meaning on the event and therefore casts her own "reality"—each reality true unto itself. Holding multiple, often conflicting realities at once is a difficult task; however, it is the developmental task all humans must strive for, if we are to embrace a more sophisticated and richer portrait of our world.

MUSICAL SELECTION

Ella Fitzgerald, "Let's Call the Whole Thing Off"

MATERIALS

Journals

A number of different images. The images can be composed of illustrations or photographs that may be taken from calendars or magazines like *National Geographic* or photo journalism publications. The images themselves should be ambiguous so that the context of the image (what the image actually is, or what is happening in the picture) could be interpreted in many different ways.

SEEING DOUBLE

INSTRUCTIONS

✳ Place girls into dyads or small groups of up to a maximum of five participants.

✳ Give one image to each group. Have participants *silently* reflect on the image. It is important that they keep their questions and comments to themselves at this time. There should be no talking.

✳ Have girls write some kind of narration in their journals that relates to the image. Encourage creativity: They may write in the form of a story or a poem. Participants may focus on the context of the image: for example, imagining what is happening in the image; what has happened in the past; and what will happen in the future. If there are people in the image, describe who they are and perhaps their relationship with one another. Participants may also choose to look at the image symbolically and write about what the image represents to them.

✳ Dedicate twenty to thirty minutes for their writing. Again, remind participants to be silent throughout the process.

✳ Once participants have finished, have groups share their stories with one another. For smaller groups, have participants share their stories with the entire group while the facilitator displays the image that they have written about. Follow up with discussion questions.

GROUP DISCUSSION

- Did anyone in your group have the exact same story?
- From what we have learned, why do you think people may experience (see) an image or even an event differently?
- How could you do this exercise focusing on conflict?
- What do you assume about another person you're in a conflict with, when they don't see something the same way you do?
- How could you deal with a conflict when you and another person may be seeing things from different perspectives?

SEEING DOUBLE

PARENT PATH

When you are with your daughter and see an ambiguous image, create an impromptu story about the image or what the image symbolically represents to you. Invite her to do the same. You can also initiate this kind of storytelling in the context of people-watching; inventing your own stories about people and then sharing them with each other. Be kind. This exercise evokes creativity, insight into another's imagination, and can sometimes elicit much-needed laughter.

SEEING DOUBLE

HERSTORY

**"If we could know the secret history of our enemies we would reveal
a grief and sorrow so great it would disarm all hostility."**
—HENRY WADSWORTH LONGFELLOW

INSPIRATION

Listening is an art; it is also a gift. We each carry to some degree the weight of our individual struggles and stressors that often feel oppressive and, at times, unbearable. When an individual is able to articulate these burdens and be truly heard, it is as if for a moment someone walks beside us and lovingly carries our burden, giving us the strength and clarity to continue on. Listening is not only an auditory function; it is taking in another's experience on an emotional and even energetic level. Listening requires patience, presence, and a capacity to hold the depths and complexities of emotion. It is one of those rare and gracious acts that can ease the heart of a fellow traveler, as well as enrich our own sense of connection with others.

MUSICAL SELECTION

Kelly Clarkson, "If No One Will Listen"

INSTRUCTIONS

✳ Talk about the function and gift of listening. Brainstorm with the group the markers of a good listener. For example: eye contact, full presence and awareness on the speaker, voice cues, attentive body language.

✳ Ask girls to get into dyads. Dyads will discuss a prompt selected by the facilitator. For the first five minutes, one participant will be the speaker and the other the listener. For the second five minutes, the girls will switch roles.

✳ The following are a few suggested discussion topics:

- **Talk about one of your most challenging life experiences.**
- **Talk about something you struggle with in your family.**
- **Talk about something that has been heavy on your mind lately.**

✳ Instruct participants who are the listener to practice being mindful and attentive to the speaker. The listener may ask the speaker questions to prompt the
speaker to go into more detail if there is space and time to do so, but the listener
should refrain from giving advice or opinions or relating their partner's narrative
to anything from their life.

✳ When the speaker has finished sharing, the listener should summarize *in her own
words* what she heard the speaker say. She may begin summarizing her partner's
story with, "So what I heard you say is . . ."

✳ After the dyads have participated as both listener and speaker, ask for volunteers
to share the stories. With permission from her partner, the volunteer may present
her partner's story in the first-person narrative, as if it was her own story.

✳ After sharing her (partner's) story, the facilitator will ask the volunteer questions
about her feelings surrounding certain aspects of the story. For example, the
facilitator might ask, "What was it like for you to . . ." or "What were you feeling
when . . ." Without consulting her partner, the volunteer will have to imagine
what her partner's experience might have been and respond to the facilitator's
questions as if it was her own experience.

GROUP DISCUSSION

- How many of you felt that your partner was really listening?
- What things did your partner do that made you feel that way?
- What was easier for you, listening or speaking, and why?
- What prevents you from being totally present when you're listening to someone?
- Who in your life listens deeply to you?
- Who do you listen to deeply and mindfully?

HERSTORY

PARENT PATH

The most frequent complaint I hear from teenagers is that their parents don't know how to listen. Deep listening requires not only giving someone the space to express themselves or utilizing reflective listening techniques, but offering curiosity and empathy as well.

Conflict with your daughter is inevitable during the adolescent years. The ability to slow down the action and use reflective listening skills can often diffuse some of the venom of these conflictual exchanges. If possible, during a conflict, stop judging and contradicting her in your head and listen to what your daughter is saying. Repeat back in your own words everything you heard her say in as much detail as possible. After summarizing, ask her if you "got it right." She will clarify if there is a need to. Infuse this type of listening and reflection as much as possible into your dialogue with her. After modeling reflective listening a few times in different conflicts, ask your daughter to do the same. When each person holds space for another's truth, whether they agree with it or not, it creates room for more understanding and less antagonism within a disagreement.

FISH BOWL

"[A human being] experiences himself, his thoughts and feelings as something
separate from the rest, a kind of optical delusion of consciousness.
This delusion is a kind of prison for us, restricting us to our personal desires
and to affection for a few persons nearest to us. Our task must be to free
ourselves from the prison by widening our circle of compassion to embrace
all living creatures and the whole of nature in its beauty . . ."
—ALBERT EINSTEIN

INSPIRATION

It is rare to have an opportunity to be given the space and time to speak one's truth
and be fully heard without interruption or judgment. It is equally special to listen to
another person's experiences when they are able to fully reveal their truth with depth
and honesty. These special moments allow folks with different backgrounds and
experiences to challenge their preconceived perceptions of others and ultimately
gain more clarity and respect for the other's reality.

MUSICAL SELECTION

Sara Bareilles, "Brave"

PREPARATION

Before forming the group, discuss what it means to be an ally to an identity group
different from your own. (An ally is a member of an advantaged social group who
works to understand their privilege and advocates for uprooting oppressive beliefs
and behaviors.) Take extra care while facilitating this activity to be sure participants
hold space for and respect each other's perspectives, resisting the urge to correct or
defend. Then, the group can be conducted in two ways.

FISH BOWL

Example #1

✳ Have the entire group sit in a circle facing one another. The facilitator will prompt the discussion with one of several questions. Here are a few suggested topics:

• **What is difficult about being a teenager?**

• **What has been your experience of being a girl?**

• **What is hard about living in your world? What do you love about it?**

Example #2

✳ The group is broken down into observers and speakers. The speakers may be from a particular identity group; for example, African American females, or those who identify with the LGBTQ community. The speakers form a small inner circle facing each other while the listeners form a circle around the speakers.

✳ The listeners may not comment on the dialogue in the inner circle at any point and should remain totally silent and attentive at all times as a sign of respect and solidarity.

✳ The facilitator then asks the inner circle a series of questions about their experiences. Below are a list of sample prompts:

• **Describe your experience as a [member of this identity group].**

• **When was the first time you realized you were [this identity group]?**

• **What do you like about being [a member]?**

• **What is challenging about being [a member]?**

• **Is there anything you would want others to know who are not [a member]?**

✳ When the discussion ends, thank the inner group for their courage and honesty and the outer group for their respect. Remind the group that they should not comment or create a rebuttal to any of the experiences expressed, or confront a particular person about something they said, then or anytime thereafter. Instead, invite group members to allow the experiences expressed to sink in and to use them as valuable information to inform and possibly adjust their perceptions of a particular identity group.

This exercise can be used for more than one identity group and may be spaced out over several days of discussions.

FISH BOWL

PARENT PATH

When you and your daughter find yourselves in a moment of contention, when possible, stop for a moment, internally drop your position as parent and adult, and enter into her world. You are not shifting your position to give in to her needs, but rather listening to understand the deeper layers of her frustration, which is generally hard to hear unless you drop your rebuttal. Then, you can use your reflective listening skills and convey to her in as much detail as possible all that you experienced by trying to place yourself in her position. You do not have to change your thinking if it still feels true. Your daughter may still be frustrated by your position, but she will feel better being truly heard, and she will learn an important lesson: that being heard doesn't necessarily mean she will always get her way. Moreover, if you are able to accomplish this state of deep listening in the midst of madness, you will inevitably discover new levels of empathy.

IN DEFENSE OF VULNERABILITY

**"We cultivate love when we allow our most vulnerable selves
to be deeply seen and known."
—BRENÉ BROWN**

OVERVIEW

✳ Life can be painful. Things are done and said to us throughout our lifetime that
can leave profound wounds. We often continue to experience these wounds
through our insecurities and fears. Instead of coming to terms with this universal
truth—that we all are wounded—we erect strategies of subterfuge and barriers of
defense to protect and conceal our wounds. By doing so, we also erect a barrier
to receiving and giving the kind of support and connection we need in order to
heal and grow.

MUSICAL SELECTION

Zara McFarlane, "Open Heart"

MATERIALS

Defensive Communication worksheet for each participant

INSTRUCTIONS

✳ Talk about the function of defensive communication and go over the Defensive
Communication worksheet together. As you review the worksheet, ask participants for examples from their lives to illustrate the different categories of defensive communication. It would be helpful for you to also have anecdotes from
your own life in case they can't come up with examples for all the terms.

✳ Have group members get into dyads, and ask each dyad to develop a scene (no
more that two minutes long) that escalates into conflict. Within the scene, each
actor will enact at least two different kinds of defensive communication.

IN DEFENSE OF

✳ Volunteer dyads will play out their scenes in front of the group. When most of the scene has been carried out, freeze the scene. The group will refer to the worksheet and try to guess which kinds of defensive communication the actors portrayed in the scene.

✳ Finally, the dyad will portray the scene again, escalating to the conflict. However, instead of continuing to use defensive communication, the actors will reveal how they feel without any defensive tactics. They may use the following phrase as a template (display somewhere in the room if possible):

"I'm feeling _____ because when you did/said _____, I interpreted that you _____.

(As the facilitator, you may have to guide participants through this process. If actors express that they feel angry, validate that feeling, and also ask them to dig deeper and see if they feel any other emotion—e.g. hurt, embarrassment, fear—that they might be experiencing. In addition, if they resort to blaming the other person, ask them to focus on how they interpreted the other person's actions or words and what insecurities and fears might have come up for them based on their interpretations.)

✳ In turn, the other actor will have a chance to clarify what they meant by their words or actions and to reveal their feelings and interpretations.

✳ Follow with discussion questions.

GROUP DISCUSSION

- What was the main difference between the two scenes?
- What kinds of defensive communication do you use most? With whom do you do this most?
- What is your biggest fear about sharing what you are really feeling with another?
- What do you think would be the effect on your relationships if you were more open with your thoughts and feelings?

VULNERABILITY

Defensive Communication worksheet

Avoiding   Behaviors that stongly try to prevent one from directly confronting feelings and issues.

Guilt-tripping   Inciting shame and guilt in others in order to avoid responsibility.

Withholding   Holding back words, emotions, and/or your presence as a form of punishment to the other party involved.

Sarcasm   A tone of voice that is intended to be belittling or condescending.

Passive-Aggressive Behavior   Instead of dealing openly with resentment or hurt, a person might do things they know will annoy or hurt another person in an indirect manner.

Joking   Rather than taking concerns seriously, a person distracts or dismisses those concerns through humor.

Counterattacking   Rather than listen and take in concerns, a person blames or criticizes.

Martyrdom   Using false humility to avoid discussing an issue with another person.

Projecting   Instead of allowing feelings to be owned and expressed, a person will unconsciously attribute their own feelings or issues to another person.

Repression / Denial   Denying to yourself and/or others feelings and experiences that are too painful to admit.

Justifying   Making arguments that do not include taking responsibility for your actions.

Mindreading   Expecting people to know what you need and then getting upset when they don't do or say what you wanted them to do or say.

PARENT PATH

One of my graduate professors once said to a class, "If you want to see perfect modeling of defensive communication, find a teenager." If you have a defensive teenage daughter, rather than call her out on her communication style, you may try hanging a copy of the Defensive Communication worksheet somewhere she'll take note of it. It is a small step toward her growing awareness of how she is communicating with others. If she brings up the worksheet, talk with her about it. It's likely that she will identify *your* defensive communication styles, so try to be open and receptive. This may also create an opportunity for you to openly address her defensive communication with a common vocabulary you both understand.

MIRROR, MIRROR

**"Unless you learn to face your own shadows,
you will continue to see them in others, because the world outside you
is only a reflection of the world inside you."**
—CARL JUNG

INSPIRATION

Projection is a psychological concept which proposes that individuals, in order to defend themselves from uncomfortable feeling states and qualities, will deny those feelings or qualities in themselves and attribute them to another person. Based on this understanding, the people we interface with can often serve as mirrors, amplified versions of ourselves reflecting what we need to reclaim and accept in ourselves.

MUSICAL SELECTION

Keke Palmer, "Man in the Mirror"

MATERIALS

Journals
Easel paper 25"x30"

INSTRUCTIONS

✳ Write the prompts that follow on a large easel paper.

✳ Ask the girls to respond to the following prompts in their journals. Encourage girls to think about the questions and to go as deeply and honestly as they can into their responses. Inform participants that this writing activity will not be shared with anyone.

  • Identify someone whose presence and/or manner deeply irritates you. Or it might be someone you feel you just don't like. Write down her name.

  • Identify what qualities about this person bother you. Be specific.

  • Imagine why this person does the things they do? Don't assume they are "just that way," or trying to be hurtful or annoying. Dig deeper.

- **Look back on the qualities that bother you most about this person. Is there anyone in your life (e.g. family, friends, peers, teachers) who might point out the same qualities or characteristics about you? Look deeply and be honest. Can you think of an example of how you have displayed a quality you don't like in this other person in your own life?**

- **At the core level, what do you imagine would help this person be a better version of themselves?**

✳ When everyone has finished writing, ask participants to close their journals and have them center themselves (closing their eyes is preferable).

✳ Ask participants to imagine standing face to face with the person they wrote about. Invite participants to try to see this person with new eyes: based on a deeper understanding of the behavior and on reflecting that this person may be pointing out something about themselves. Ask them to look into the eyes of the other with genuine compassion and say the words "I wish you peace and happiness." When they can imagine this exchange with sincerity, they may open their eyes.

CIRCLE DISCUSSION

✳ Follow up with a discussion in small groups or one large group. Have girls talk about what came up for them from this exercise. Make sure that the girls do not disclose the names of people they focused on for the exercise.

PARENT PATH

Inevitably, as a parent you will occasionally become irritated with your teenage daughter. During one of these moments, it may be helpful to employ this exercise yourself. Write down your responses to the suggested prompts above. Try to be detailed and reflective. Conclude the writing exercise with some version of the visualization suggested above. If done sincerely, this exercise has the ability to shift you out of irritation and give you more insight and compassion into your daughter and the situation at hand.

GOLD DIGGER

**"Trouble is a part of your life, and if you don't share it, you don't give
the person who loves you enough chance to love you enough."**
—DINAH SHORE

INSPIRATION

In some acting classes, a drama teacher or coach will often shout out to the actors,
"What is your character's motivation? What does she want?" The idea behind this is
that human words and actions are usually motivated by a need. And our needs reveal
a deeper truth about ourselves. Unfortunately, we often have shame around some of
our needs—to belong or be acknowledged, respected, autonomous, or nurtured—
and thus we hide those needs from others. It is this fact alone that creates so much
conflict and misunderstanding among people. When we can dig past the subterfuge
of language and false personages that hide our needs, we create a golden moment
when we allow ourselves and others to express genuine needs, and thereby have a
chance to get those needs met.

MUSICAL SELECTION

Ani DiFranco, "As Is"

MATERIALS

Paper and pens

INSTRUCTIONS

✳ Discuss with the girls the ideas presented in the overview. There are different
categories of needs. You may want to expose participants to the psychologist
Abraham Maslow's helpful diagram illustrating the "Hierarchy of Needs." In addition, present the idea that in communication there is often:

Presentation   Surface words, actions, and feelings.

Underlying need   A need or desire that is unspoken.

✳ Present an example of a dialogue that has both presentation and underlying motivations or needs:

Mother: How was your day?

Daughter: Pretty good. I got a B on my oral exam.

Mother: Hmm.

Daughter: I'm going up to my room; let me know when dinner is ready.

Mother: Is that the exam you waited until the last minute to study for?

Daughter: (sarcastically) Yes, it's the same one I asked you to help test me on, but you didn't have time.

Mother: (sarcastically) Excuse me. I work incredibly hard for you and me to have food on the table. I'm sorry I wasn't available at that moment!

Daughter: Whatever. I'm going to go up to my room. I'm going to have dinner there!

Mother: No, you won't! You're going to eat at the table, young lady.

Daughter pouts, and runs up to her room.

✳ Discuss line by line the underlying need of each exchange between mother and daughter. For example:

Mother: How was your day? (Desire to connect)

Daughter: Pretty good. I got a B on my oral exam. (Need for positive acknowledgment)

Mother: Hmm. (Judgment without openly disclosing feeling or thoughts)

Daughter: I'm going up to my room; let me know when dinner is ready. (Display of disconnection and underlying feelings of anger or disappointment at her mother's response and perhaps shame that she didn't live up to her mother's expectations)

Mother: Is that the exam you waited until the last minute to study for? (Punishing/shaming daughter because she didn't get her own expectations met, i.e., grades/to connect)

Daughter: Yes, it's the same one I ask you to help test me on, but you didn't have time. (Retaliation: Punishing/shaming)

Mother: Excuse me. I work incredibly hard for you and me to have food on the table. I'm sorry I wasn't available at that moment! (Guilting and need for acknowledgment)

Daughter: Whatever. I'm going to go up to my room. I'm going to have dinner there! (Needing to disconnect perhaps because dialogue has become too hurtful, exhibiting power to shut down connection)

Mother: No, you won't! You're going to eat at the table, young lady. (Reestablishing power)

Daughter pouts and runs up to her room. (Passive aggressive reassertion of power, need for safety)

✳ Create a new dialogue with the group, based on the genuine motivation and needs of the characters. In other words, each character will state her needs honestly and up front. For example:

Mother: How was your day?

Daughter: Pretty good. I got a B on my oral exam.

Mother: Hmm.

Daughter: I'm going up to my room; let me know when dinner is ready.

Mother: I'm sorry, did that seem judgmental? What I was thinking was 'Wow, she got a B! AND that was the test she waited until the last minute to study for'. I guess I'm pleasantly surprised you did well even though I wasn't sure if you had even studied for it. I was also wondering what would have happened if you had studied more for it.

Daughter: I asked you for help earlier, but I guess I could have done better.

Mother: You did ask me, and I told you I would help you after I had finished with my work, but you got angry and that was the end of it. You did really well on your own. I just need you to be a little more flexible with me. I'm juggling a lot of things right now and I feel bad when I can't do it all . . . like I'm failing you. You've really been handling your responsibilities well and I'm proud of you and I just want you to do your best.

Daughter: I hear you. I just get hurt when you're not there for me. I feel like I don't matter at that moment. I just get anxious about stuff and I feel I need help and I give up if I don't get it.

Mother: Aw honey, I totally get that. Thank you for telling me. I'll try to be more present and sensitive to that at the time. I guess both of us feel anxious at times and we need a little compassion from the people around us.

✳ Have girls get into dyads. The dyads will work together to create and write a dialogue between two people that contains a "presentation" and also "underlying needs." The dialogues may be based on a real occasion or made up, and should be around five to ten lines long.

✳ The dyads will also create a secondary dialogue that will openly express each character's actual needs and feelings. Have participants use the first few lines of

GOLD DIGGER

the original dialogue until the point when the conflict begins to surface, and from then on they can create new dialogue.

* Volunteer dyads will perform their first dialogues and follow this by facilitating a group discussion having the group try to identify the unspoken needs of each of the characters in the dialogue. Finally, the dyad will perform the second dialogue for the group.

* Follow volunteer dyad performances with a group discussion.

GROUP DISCUSSION:

- **Why do you think people hide their true needs and desires from others?**
- **What is so difficult about being vulnerable?**
- **What does it feel like when a person is vulnerable and honest with you about their thoughts, feelings, and needs?**
- **If you were to pinpoint a need(s) that is most important to you, what would it be? Examples: Need to belong or to be respected, acknowledged, or nurtured; to express yourself; to have freedom.**

PARENT PATH

Looking deeper into the motivating forces that are directing you and your daughter's words and actions is crucial if you want to reveal what you're really fighting about. Below the surface of some more superficial arguments lie needs that are not being addressed. The more you are able to both address and express the real needs in a given situation or in a relationship in general, the more successful you will be at genuinely solving the issue and repairing the relationship you have with your daughter.

Ask yourself when you are in conflict with your daughter what you need that you're not expressing, and whether it is fair to ask your daughter to fulfill those needs. For instance, in the example above the mother sarcastically states: *"Excuse me, I work incredibly hard for you and me to have food on the table. I'm sorry I wasn't available at that moment!"*

Underneath the surface of the mother's words, she may have been trying, in part, to guilt her daughter. But why? What does she truly want? Perhaps to be acknowledged for being a single mother trying to do the best she can. Is it then fair to ask her daughter to fulfill that need? Maybe, but if the mother/daughter relationship has been too enmeshed, and the mother has inappropriately looked to her daughter to provide her with a sense of purpose and worth, then the daughter will eventually (and justifiably) refuse to do so and that will likely take the form of aggression and distance.

> Conversely, the daughter wants space from her mother (*"I'm going up to my room; let me know when dinner is ready"*) and on the contrary wants her mother's attention (*"Yes, it's the same one I ask you to help test me on, but you didn't have time"*). This is both confusing and lacking in empathy for her mother's effort and struggle. It is an illustration of the contrasting needs to on the one hand be connected to her mother and on the other to gain independence from her.

When you and your daughter are in clearer frames of mind and not entangled in a surface argument, ask your daughter what she needs from you. Help her define her needs by narrowing them down: need for nurturing, need to be acknowledged, need to feel safe, need for autonomy, need for your undivided attention. Explain to her that she may have different needs at the same time or at different moments. Try to head off large-scale conflicts by asking your daughter to identify what she *really* needs. It is important that you model the same transparency you want from her. If you come to the conclusion that a particular need you have is something that may not be fair to be asking of her, then express that to her as well.

It is important to learn that everyone has needs and that those needs may be conflicting—and that they may not always be able to be met by another person. However, by voicing your deeper needs, you establish clarity, self-respect, emotional intimacy, and a much clearer path to getting your needs met.

BOUNDARY CHECK*

"When you say 'yes' to others make sure you are not saying 'no' to yourself."
—PAULO COELHO

INSPIRATION

We teach people, moment by moment, how to treat us by letting them know what we will and won't allow. When we remain silent about our needs or what hurts us, we betray ourselves; we reinforce to ourselves that we don't deserve to have a voice. Speaking up on our own behalf is a form of self-love and an invitation to others to love us as we want to be loved.

MUSICAL SELECTION

Tori Amos, "Silent All These Years"

INSTRUCTIONS

✷ Participants get into dyads.

✷ Have the dyads face each other with at least ten feet of space between them.

✷ Instruct each participant to come up with things that she likes or would like to have happen, and have her propose these things to her partner. For example:

"I like sushi; do you?"

"I would like to go swimming; do you want to go?"

"I like that jacket you're wearing; can I borrow it?"

✷ With each offer, participants are asked to check in with themselves as to whether, they *genuinely* like or want to do what is being proposed. The facilitator should emphasize to participants that they reflect on *their* needs and desires and not on pleasing their partner. Participants will then respond to the offer by saying "Yes" and moving forward a step toward their partner, or by saying "No" and taking a step backward.

✷ Dyads should take turns asking and responding. The activity can last up to fifteen minutes. Follow up with discussion questions.

GROUP DISCUSSION

• Talk about what feelings came up for you when you said "yes" or "no" to your partner in response to their propositions. Did you feel empowered? Did you feel worried about their feelings?

• When you make decisions that include others, do you think of others' desires or your own? Which usually wins out?

• Talk about a time when you said yes to something you didn't want to do, or no to something you really wanted to do.

• Why do you think it may be hard for some girls to say no to others?

• How could setting one's boundaries (saying no) be positive?

• What may be a consequence of saying "no" to others?

• How could asking for what you want be a positive thing to do?

• What may be a consequence of asking for what you want?

*Modified from an exercise of Amy Jo Goddard

BOUNDARY CHECK

PARENT PATH

Setting restrictions and boundaries with teenagers is a balancing act. On the one hand, teenagers often feel overwhelmed by the circumstances and emotions that surround them daily. They secretly desire security and stability and a parent's solid "no"; as much as teens may resist, they often gain the sense of containment they need from firm boundaries. However, parents often, out of fears for their children's well being and out of a habit of being the one in control, overuse their "no" power to the detriment of their child's development. While teenagers need some boundaries, their developmental task is that of autonomy and individuation, and however hard it is, parents must learn to begin to let go and trust the teen's process, including some mistakes they *will* make.

The next time you're confronted with a request from your child to do something, check in with yourself. What does your gut (not fear or a need for control) say to you? Think of these requests from your child as opportunities to expand her world and an opportunity for you to illustrate your trust in her. When it still doesn't feel right or safe, establish a firm "no" and be consistent with your stance. The more good decision-making and responsibility your daughter exhibits, the more you can loosen the reins and increase her independence.

BOUNDARY CHECK

MEDIA ROUNDTABLE

"The most beautiful people we have known are those who have known defeat, known suffering, known struggle, known loss, and have found their way out of the depths. These persons have an appreciation, a sensitivity, and an understanding of life that fills them with compassion, gentleness, and a deep loving concern. Beautiful people do not just happen."
—ELISABETH KÜBLER-ROSS

INSPIRATION

Empathy is a powerful vehicle for change. When we witness a person's reality and it moves our heart, it awakens compassion, virtue, and even rage. It is from these feelings that action is born. With the growth of progressive and independent media, we have more and more opportunities to document and witness worlds vastly different from our own and thus greater opportunities to activate our heart and take action for change.

MUSICAL SELECTION

Eryn Allen Kane, "Have Mercy"

MATERIALS

Video screen/DVD player or Internet access
Selected movie (See suggestions)

PREPARATION

Review movie ahead of time and come up with discussion questions for the group
    to dialogue about after the movie has been presented.

INSTRUCTIONS

✳ Select a documentary that covers a topical issue that is not only informative
but also poignant. Provided below are a few suggestions of documentary titles;
however you may choose from your catalogue of favorites, while being careful to
ensure the film's content is age-appropriate for your group.

>SUGGESTIONS:
>
>**Girl Rising**
>
>**My Flesh and Blood**
>
>**Bully**
>
>**Revolution**
>
>**Miss Representation**
>
>**Invisible Children**
>
>**Children Underground**
>
>**The Cove**
>
>**Blackfish**
>
>**Darwin's Nightmare**
>
>**Food Inc.**
>
>**Earthlings**

The film may be watched all at once or broken down into two sittings, but
leave at least thirty minutes for a discussion that will follow the film.

GROUP DISCUSSION

✳ Have the girls sit in a circle and discuss their thoughts and feelings about the
documentary. Use discussion prompts to initiate dialogue if the discussion seems
to be coming to an end. Some sample discussion questions are provided, but
you may want to come up with your own that are more specific to the particular
movie that you present.

Sample discussion questions:

- **What part of the movie stood out to you most?**
- **What happens to you physically and emotionally when you witness (oppression, cruelty, injustice)?**
- **Have you ever acted when you felt a great sense of injustice? What happened?**

MEDIA ROUNDTABLE

PARENT PATH ....

Movies are sometimes one of the last connections available for teenagers and their parents during a strained adolescent period. Establish weekly movie nights and incorporate informative and moving documentaries or movies. Afterward, together share your thoughts and feelings about the movie. You may incorporate the sample discussion questions provided above or create your own. When sharing your own thoughts avoid lecturing about "the point" of the movie. Stay curious about and open to your daughter's ideas.

MEDIA ROUNDTABLE

4

NECESSARY ACTION

In one of the first adolescent groups I ran, I showed a documentary on the exploitation and abuse of girls around the globe. It was not an easy film to watch. I warned the girls ahead of time of the film's content, but they were of course intrigued and insisted on watching it. As the film came to a close and the closing credits appeared, I turned on the lights in the room. The girls looked despondent and listless. I thought that perhaps the documentary had bored them. One of the girls excused herself and walked outside the door and stood there, looking up at the sky. The other girls remained silent.

I couldn't quite read the pulse of the room, so I walked up to the front of the classroom and asked, "Questions, comments? What's going on?" The girls stared at me for a moment and then Keisha, a bright and spirited young woman, broke the silence. "So this is going on right now?" I responded, "Yes, as we sit and breathe." She looked at me, incredulous and disgusted, and asked, "Why isn't anyone doing anything?" I paused before responding, knowing I couldn't give her an answer that would fully satisfy her. "People are doing things. This documentary is shedding light on the issue so that more people are aware of what's going on." "That's not enough!" a girl named Tania blurted out. "These women are suffering now!" Girls' voices then emerged throughout the room, a cacophony of outrage. "If so many people now know, why is it still happening? We should buy some plane tickets and go out there and do something. I know someone here who had that happen to her. This world is so wack!" I stood there and took this all in. The group's animated reactions elicited two responses within me. On the one hand, I feel and understand the girls' raw anger. They were right: How do we as a people, once we are aware of the injustice and violence that exist in the world, not turn wild with disgust, rage, and disappointment? For a

moment, I want to scream or cry, or walk out, look up at the sky, and demand to
square off with the powers that be for an explanation. And then, almost imme-
diately, my adult response kicks in, a numbing that begins in my head with the
words, "Calm down; it's a much more complicated issue. There are barriers and
practicalities. These things are very difficult to change . . ." Instead, I turn to
these ignited warriors with tears in my eyes and say to them, "You're right to be
angry. What do you want to do about it?"

☾   ✳   ☾

One of the startling moments in the adolescent years is the revelation of all the
injustice and cruelty that exist in the world. It's not that these things did not exist
before, obviously, but frequently a child is, justifiably, shielded from worldly atroc-
ities, and even in the case that they are not shielded, the child's mind often doesn't
quite comprehend the full impact of the brutality they have seen or experienced.
During adolescence, the veil of childhood is lifted, and what is revealed is a much
less idealistic, more balanced portrait of life. Adolescent youth often feel betrayed,
disappointed, and angry about this reality; however, the discovery is also an invitation to fully and genuinely enter the world and, if one feels so compelled, become
an agent of change in that environment. When adults try to hide the shadow of the
world, we are indirectly telling young minds and hearts that the injustices they see
around them aren't real or do not matter, and that young people have no power
to influence or change their environment. If the injustices of this world are to be
dismantled, it will be because each generation becomes more exposed to them and
more invested in and empowered to changing them.

I believe social engagement is a necessary and powerful component of youth
development. It enlarges teenagers' perspective of the world, often leading to
greater empathy and humility; it provides an arena to develop their ability to affect
their environment; it allows them to channel both their idealism and anger in a
life-affirming manner; and it provides the forces of change—a new and inspired
energy that helps to fuel the ongoing struggle against injustice, greed, and violence.

Social engagement takes empathy a step further, by not only trying to understand another's suffering but also acting to alleviate it. Social engagement is considered by many social scientists the highest form of social competence and is

considered to be a "transformative" adaptive response that is linked to resiliency.[1] Moreover, social engagement supports young people by enabling them to develop an "oppositional gaze" in their awareness of the nature of oppression, whether inflicted by an abusive parent or a sexist society, and offering strategies for overcoming those injustices rather than being victimized by them.[2]

Necessary Action briefly exposes girls to some of the current issues facing women around the world in the twenty-first century (Lighthouses). Participants are then encouraged, through a series of activities, to enter into their world with the goal of affecting change (Random Acts of Kindness, Parts I and II). Finally, the girls will identify people, personal skills, and interests that inspire ideas for transformative and creative work in their futures (Shero and Envisioning Purpose).

1   P. Oliner and S. Oliner, *The Roots of Altruism* (New York: American Jewish Committee, 1989).
    G. Vallant, "Adaptive mental mechanics: their role in positive psychology," *American Psychologist* 55 (2002): 89-98.
2   bell hooks, *Black Looks: Race and Representation* (Boston: South End Press, 1992).

LIGHTHOUSES

"The way to right wrongs is to turn the light of truth upon them."
—IDA B. WELLS

INSPIRATION

Great strides have been made toward creating more freedom and equality for women in the last century. Women have become increasingly more powerful in the political, economic, and professional arenas. However, these gains can often act as a silk screen to the misogyny and sexism that still exist within the United States and around the world. Young women are invited—in order to know both the power of their birthright, as well as the violence committed against them—to have a more balanced and mature understanding of what struggles females face in the twenty-first century.

MUSICAL SELECTION

Natalie Merchant, "My Skin"

MATERIALS

Sticky easel paper 25"x30"

PREPARATION

On a sheet of easel paper write a list of suggested topics that girls can do a project on. See the sample list on page 121.

INSTRUCTIONS

⋆ Discuss some of the struggles that participants believe females face.

⋆ After the discussion, reveal the list of topics (make sure there are more topics than participants). Participants will be asked to reflect and then to choose a topic by writing their name next to the female-centered issue of their choice (one topic per participant).

The project will consist of two parts:

The Facts An informal, brief report explaining: what is the issue; who or what is being affected; who is the perpetrator; where is this taking place; what are the underlying reasons; and any noteworthy statistics on the issue. This presentation can be anywhere from two to five minutes long.

Creative Expression Participants will create some form of artistic representation that personalizes the issue they are featuring. The following are a few examples of creative media, but participants may express their topic however they choose:

Poem	Music and/or a song
Media piece	Story
Dance piece	Collage
Painting	Sculpture

✱ Here is a list of suggested topics. Feel free to add more.

Anorexia/bulimia	Beauty standard for girls and women
Depression among females	Sexual/gender orientation and violence
Sex trade in the United States	Sex trade abroad
Sexual terrorism	Female infanticide
Female genital mutilation	Marriage by abduction
Domestic violence	Rape on college campuses
Ecofeminism (the link between violence against the earth/nature with violence against women)	

GROUP DISCUSSION

✱ After each presentation, group members should be encouraged to ask questions to each presenter about the topic that was presented.

PARENT PATH

It is important to expose your daughter to current social and political issues, because when she is informed, her world expands and she becomes aware of truths that draw her out of her own tragedies and bring forth humility and awareness. You might start by focusing on issues that may be relevant to or of interest to your daughter. If you can, take her occasionally to a lecture or a protest that you think she could process and would hold her interest. Cut out articles weekly around issues she may be interested in, or stories of people and/or organizations impacting key issues. Pin these articles on a corkboard in the kitchen or by the toilet. Avoid proselytizing; just give her the opportunity for exposure and let her connect to what she feels drawn to. The larger and more important message you're sending is that outside her adolescent sphere there is a world that exists and matters.

RANDOM ACTS OF KINDNESS, PART I

"If the world is to be healed through human effort, I am convinced it will be by ordinary people. People whose love for this life is even greater than their fear."
—JOANNA MACY

INSPIRATION

Kindness directed toward a stranger is a subtle yet revolutionary act toward transforming our society. It is a compassionate deed that is not only supportive to another; it is also a radical interruption of a cultural ethos that often centers around selfishness. In one spontaneous act of kindness, we are promoting a world in which we acknowledge others, where resources and assistance are abundant, and trust, empathy, and generosity are valued more than fear and self-interest. Through all our acts, however big or small, we are creating the world we wish to live in.

MUSICAL SELECTION

Jane Siberry, "Calling All Angels"

INSTRUCTIONS

✳ *(Optional)* Have the group watch the movie *Pay It Forward*.

✳ Initiate a discussion with group members about a time in which a stranger or someone they barely knew did something kind for them without any expectation of something in return.

✳ Assign participants the task of going out into their world and doing something kind and unexpected for a stranger or someone they do not know very well.

The deed may be planned or spontaneous. Participants should not explain at any point that the deed was done as an assignment nor should they expect to get something in return.

✳ Examples of kind acts follow, but participants are encouraged to come up with their own:

> **Pay for someone's bus fare.**
>
> **Give someone a flower, or smile and walk away.**
>
> **Strike up a conversation with someone who looks lonely or sad.**
>
> **Assist an elderly person walking or carrying something.**
>
> **Genuinely compliment someone on a quality, talent, or feature that makes him or her special.**

✳ At the next session, have each member share their experience with the group:

- **Whom did they approach?**
- **What was the deed?**
- **What response did they get?**
- **How did they feel afterward?**

PARENT PATH

Parents often talk to their children about the merits of trust, kindness, and compassion, but sometimes paint a very different picture through their own actions. Ask yourself: How do you interact with the world? Are you warm and open to strangers, or cautious and private? Do you help those in need? If so, what is the manner or limit of your engagement? More than any philosophical sermon you could give your daughter, these subtle interactions tell her much more clearly what you truly believe about the world and an individual's role within it.

∪

RANDOM ACTS OF KINDNESS, PART II

"Activism is my rent for living on this planet."
—ALICE WALKER

INSTRUCTIONS

The facilitator can organize this activity in several different ways:

1. Each participant can identify a cause and local organization for which they can volunteer for a day (ideally anywhere from three to six hours). Participants will then come back and report on the issue and their volunteer experiences.

OR

2. The facilitator identifies an organization that the group can work with together. The organization should be one that is working on an issue that may be of interest to the girls, and that can handle multiple volunteers. The facilitator will be responsible for:

   Coordinating the day and time with the organization.

   Identifying what specific support the girls would provide that day.

   Organize transportation (Ask parents for transportation assistance or coordinate with bus/metro schedule).

   Prep group members beforehand about the issue the organization focuses on, along with any logistical information about volunteering.

Debrief the experience at the following session by having group members go around and express what observations, feelings, and comments they had regarding the issue and/or experience.

OR

3. Those participants, who so choose, can identify a cause and an organization that they would like the group to fundraise for. Participants will be given until the next session to identify the cause and organization and prepare a strong argument about why members should pick their organization.

Once all participating group members have made their plea, everyone will vote, with one caveat; participants cannot vote for their own organization, and need to select from the other identified organizations. The facilitator will tally the votes and announce the organization that received the most votes.

Have the group begin to brainstorm about how to fundraise. Write all the suggestions on a 25"x30" easel paper(s). Remind girls to be realistic and only commit to something they are able and willing to do together. Intention and completion are key here.

If the group can reach a consensus on how to fundraise, great! Part of the activity is about working as a group and they may come up with whatever solution makes sense. If an agreement cannot be made, use the voting method previously mentioned.

Once a fundraising method has been decided, set up the following organizational tools:

Brainstorm Brainstorm a step-by-step process of carrying out the fundraising. Also think about the materials the group will need and discuss who will buy the materials. With what money? Also brainstorm any possible challenges and work them out as a group.

Map Out Logistics Outline everything that needs to happen before, during, and after fundraising.

Timeline Designate dates for each task.

Assign Duties Assign group members to the various duties that have been mapped out in the timeline.

Once the project has been executed, and the contribution has been presented to the organization (if possible, present photos of the girls during the fundraising process), come together and discuss the process of the project. Group members can reflect about what worked and didn't work, as well as any impact the project had on them. Have them focus on the process and not group members. Leave time for participants to give positive feedback to each other regarding their individual efforts at the end of the session.

SHERO

**When an interviewer asked Florence Nightingale what had been
the motivating factor behind her immensely productive work
in the hospitals, she responded with one word: "Rage."**

INSPIRATION

A creative-change agent is any person who manifests change in the world through
her own creative gift. She may create breathtaking beauty in her environment, fight
against injustice with song, exhibit kindness and humor in her interactions with others, heal through art, teach with vivacity and ingenuity, or provide a depth of perspective that makes others see the world more magically. Whatever her individual
work may be in the world, it is done with a spirit of originality and excellence, transforming her environment in the process.

MUSICAL SELECTION

Sheila Chandra, "La Sagesse"

MATERIALS

One copy of the Interview Guidelines and the Shero Interview Questions worksheets
for each participant.

INSTRUCTIONS

✳ Discuss the idea of a creative-change agent. The facilitator should talk about an
   inspiring female creative-change agent that they have identified and can talk
   about. The creative-change agent does not have to be famous; she can be someone you met once or may be a family member or friend.

✳ Participants will identify their own female creative-change agent and do a small
   interview with her. Encourage participants to select someone they have access
   to in person or via phone or email. Otherwise they may have to do a bit of rigor-
   ous research to uncover more personal information required for this activity—it's
   up to them.

* Pass out the Interview Guidelines and Shero Interview Questions worksheets. Let participants know when the presentations will take place (give participants about a week or two to set up and conduct an interview or do research). Review Interview Guidelines with participants and make sure they understand how to set up and conduct their interviews.

* Let participants know they will individually present the responses they collected from the interview to the group; however, the facilitator will be the interviewer and the participant will characterize and respond to the interview questions *as if she were the change agent they selected.* Participants should attempt to embody their selected change agent in any way they can: through dress, props, mannerisms, and especially the narrative responses of their change agent.

* Each interview should take approximately five to ten minutes. After the interview, all group members are encouraged to ask the "distinguished guest" questions. The featured participant will respond to the best of her ability as the change agent.

PARENT PATH

If you haven't done so already, have a dialogue with your daughter and find out:

> What women inspire her, both well-known figures and people she knows or has met?

> What qualities inspire her about these women?

> What can she identify in herself that is reflected in the women she admires?

> If she were to use a talent(s) and/or skill(s) to change something, what would it be?

After the dialogue, collect images and words from magazines that reflect her responses. Make a collage out of the words and images and surprise her with it by hanging it up somewhere in her room.

Interview Guidelines worksheet

1. Obtain the phone number or email address of the woman you want to interview. If you don't have her direct phone number, use your network or the Internet to obtain contact information.

2. Email or phone your creative-change agent and ask to set up an interview with you by phone or in person. Here is a sample of your first contact:

   Hello, my name is _____. I am participating in a special girl's group and we were given an assignment to identify and interview a woman who really inspires us and who we consider a "creative-change agent." I really thought about it and I selected you because _____. I am wondering if you would be willing to be interviewed for my project."

3. If you are both able to do the interview in person, set up a date and time. A public space like a café or park is ideal to do the interview. If you are doing the interview by phone, set up a time and date and make clear that you will call her at the time you arranged—and make sure you do so! If she is not able to do either, ask if you can email the questions to her and that she respond by a particular date.

4. If you are able to get an interview in person, bring a recording device (most smartphones have a recorder) and ask permission to record the interview.

5. At the beginning of the interview, be prepared to share a little about yourself. Most people appreciate learning about others and it makes the interview more special for both parties.

6. During the interview, if new questions come to mind, ask them!

7. At the end of the interview, thank your interviewee and let her know once again what you appreciate about her presence and/or work in the world.

Shero Interview Questions worksheet

What is your name?

Can you describe your work?

How long have you been doing this work?

What was the initial motivation or personal experience(s) that led you to this work?

What has been the greatest challenge or barrier?

What have been your greatest success and rewards?

How do you take care of yourself, or rather how do you stay healthy mentally, emotionally, and spiritually?

If there were one main lesson you learned about yourself or about life in general that you could impart to young women, what would it be?

ENVISIONING PURPOSE

"There is no greater gift you can give or receive than to honor your calling. It's why you were born and how you become most truly alive."

—OPRAH WINFREY

INSPIRATION

Each individual comes into this world with unique gifts that are tied to a "calling," and that each member of the community is obliged to identify and pursue their calling. An individual often brushes up against their calling for the first time during their youth, sometimes in the form of a special talent or interest that takes root. If one honors their calling, it is considered a blessing, for not only is the community enriched, but the individual also becomes imbued with a sense of fullness and energy in living out their purpose.

MUSICAL SELECTION

Alicia Keys, "Girl on Fire"

MATERIALS

Sticky easel pad 25"x 30"

Felt pens for each participant

INSTRUCTIONS

✱ Have each participant come up and get an easel sheet. Participants will fold the sheet vertically in half to create a crease in the middle of the sheet. On the top left side of the sheet, they will write "Skills and Talents." On the top right half of the sheet, they will write "Interests." Make sure there is plenty of room at the bottom of the page for one more category that participants will write in later.

Skills and Talents | Interests

* Ask participants to identify at least seven of their strongest skills and talents, and write them under the heading "Skills and Talents." They may include skills and talents in:

  The arts (drawing, painting, acting, music, writing, design, and other arts or crafts)

  Athletics (all sports, including dance)

  Academics (strong memorization, critical thinking skills, strong math, language, or science skills)

  Interpersonal skills (can articulate thoughts and feelings well to others, strong mediation/conflict resolution skills, highly empathetic, charismatic)

  Intrapersonal skills (intuitive, self-aware, self-disciplined, manages feelings well)

* Participants will then write down at least seven things they have interest in or love doing, under the heading "Interests." Have them think outside the box. This could include anything: playing a sport, arranging flowers, spending time with pets, daydreaming, music. The sky's the limit!

* Next, have participants get in to groups of three or four members.

* Participants in each group will take turns presenting their sheet of skills/talents and interests. The group will then brainstorm various careers involving combinations of the two categories (talents/skills and interest). Encourage groups to think outside of the traditional career box. If the participant is curious or excited about a career suggestion, they may write it down on the bottom part of the sheet. They are also free to generate ideas along with the group. Each group member should be given approximately ten minutes for group brainstorming.

ENVISIONING PURPOSE

PARENT PATH

The activity above is ideal for doing one-on-one with your daughter. After she has generated a list of skills, talents, and interests, you can suggest other skills, talents, and interests that she may have missed or underestimated. After you both have brainstormed about different jobs/careers, you may take it one step further. If there is a path your daughter seemed particularly excited about during the brainstorm, and you know someone in your network of friends and family doing something similar in scope, arrange a day where she could visit at the job site. Give your daughter a list of questions, like those offered below, that she can discover while she is at the site visit:

How much education would you need for this kind of work?

What personal qualities and skills would you need for this kind of work?

What would you be contributing to others by doing this work?

What would be the most rewarding thing about doing this type work?

What would be most challenging?

What is your definition of success? How successful would you be if you did this type of work?

5

SACRED LIVING

As a preteen in Los Angeles, when I complained of heat exhaustion during the hot summer months, I often walked barefoot three blocks from my home to what my mother glibly described as "the biggest swimming pool in the world," also known as the Pacific Ocean. I would occasionally stand at the shore and stare in rapture at the waves. Something in the ocean pulled my heart forward. I yearned and expanded. This was one of my first encounters with love. Without any pubertal pride, I would stretch out my hands toward the ocean; I felt I could raise the waves up and crash them down, because it loved me back.

For as long as I can remember, I have understood that I was a part of something greater than what I could see—a numinous world that existed at once in me, around me, and beyond me. I experienced this transcendent rapture everywhere: in all the "houses" of the different spiritual traditions I was exposed to early as a young girl, but also when I allowed myself to be absorbed by nature or stirred by moving music, in the stillness of meditation, through tears in times of loss, and when my gratitude for something or someone pierced open my heart.

My spiritual connection was one of my greatest saving graces in my adolescent years. It created contrast and balance with the often narcissistic and materialistic culture I saw around me, and it provided a wide-angle lens through which to view my challenges and decisions. In my darkest moments, I would settle myself at the shore of the ocean or at the base of a tree or underneath the covers of my bed and give in to my tears. It was in those moments that I felt held by a metapresence that had no form or name but that I felt clearly and viscerally. This presence communicated support and guidance, not through actual words but through internal stirrings that I liked to call "heart wind." I knew in those moments that I was not alone, that I was connected to something deep and infinite—and that made all the difference.

☾   ✳   ☾

As an adult working with adolescents, I find that spirituality comes up often. In classrooms and in counseling sessions, young people, without solicitation, bring up their questions, ideas, and struggles around spiritual themes. They are hungry for depth of thought and experience, and often it is their spiritual beliefs and connection that allow them to access wisdom and security when everything in their world appears bleak.

In a national survey of about 90,000 adolescents between thirteen and eighteen years of age, the National Longitudinal Study of Adolescent Health found that spirituality is a protective factor against a variety of adolescent risk behaviors (e.g., suicide, violence, pregnancy).[3] Other research has found that people who are able to associate spiritual meaning with personal adversity are less depressed and have less anxiety.[4] The evidence shows that young people fare better, both physically and psychologically, by having some form of belief system beyond the secular.

This chapter is not intended to teach or promote any belief system or practice, but rather to help participants see the world through an expanded lens and to facilitate a spiritual connection for those who feel drawn to that realm. As the facilitator, it is important for you to model respect for the variety of spiritual traditions and practices you will explore in this chapter as well as acknowledge the communities and cultures where those traditions and practices originated. Sacred Living begins by experimenting with practices such as mindfulness (Here and Now, Natural Mystic, The Voice Within) and gratitude (Being Grateful). In addition, some of the activities will challenge participants to go beyond what is experienced through the five senses and have them explore more esoteric themes such as symbolism, ancestors, and an interfaith investigation of spiritual concepts (Reading Crow, The Love of Thousands, Spiritual Mosaic). Finally, participants will explore and creatively express their own ideas around existential topics and identify what is sacred to them (The BIG Questions, Beans, Sacred Box).

3   Kathleen Mullan Harris, *The National Longitudinal Study of Adolescent Health* (Chapel Hill, NC: University of North Carolina at Chapel Hill, 2009).

4   A. Maton & E. Wells, "Religion as a community resource for well-being: Prevention, Healing, and Empowering Pathways." *Journal of Social Issues* 51 (1995): 177–193.
    K. Pargament and A. Mahoney. "Spirituality: Discovering and Conserving the Sacred," *Handbook of Positive Psychology* (New York: Oxford Press 2002) 646–659.

BEANS

"There is a hunger for ordinary bread, and there is a hunger for love, for kindness, for thoughtfulness; and this is the great poverty that makes people suffer so much."
—MOTHER THERESA

INSPIRATION

A Hawaiian story told to me by Hank Wesselman, a Hawaiian shaman, teaches that every child who comes into this world has a bowl of perfect light. If the child lives from their center and honors their light, they will grow in strength, wisdom, and ability. If, however, the child does things against their light's nature or experiences feelings like hate, fear, jealousy, doubt, and judgment, a stone is dropped into their bowl of light. Every stone that is dropped obscures some of the light in their bowl. If the child continues to collect stones in their bowl, the light eventually goes out—and they turn into a stone. However, when the child is ready, all that the child would need to do is practice *kalana*—forgiveness for oneself and others—turn the bowl upside down, and let all the stones fall out.

In the course of a human life, some experiences and events will inevitably lead us away from our highest nature. It is important to remember, however, that the core essence of who we are is exquisite and whole; and, perhaps just knowing this is one of the essential ways of bringing us back to our light.

MUSICAL SELECTION

Trevor Hall, "Bowl of Life"

MATERIALS

One large bowl
Two small (clear) glass cups
At least two pounds of dried beans

PREPARATION

✳ Place all the beans in the large bowl

INSTRUCTIONS

The narration below is broken up into two parts: The instructions are stated first. What the facilitator should say is stated in bold italics; the facilitator may use their own words; the narration below is only a guideline.

✶ Display the bowl of beans and one of the empty glasses.

> *"We come into this world pure: filled with light and unobstructed by any fears or wounds. Like this empty glass, our body is our container and the state of being empty is, in this case, a state of wholeness, of clear consciousness without pain, doubt, or fear. Through the course of life, however, because life is not perfect, things happen to us that begin to fill our glass, make us heavier, and obstruct our true essence. For example: Your parents divorce . . ."*

✶ Take several beans out of the bowl and put them in the glass. Continue to take small handfuls out of the bowl and put them in the glass each time a violation is mentioned.

> *"You get bullied at school. You judge and feel envious of others because you think they have something that you don't."*

BEANS

✳ Ask participants to give other examples. Put a few beans into the glass every time someone from the group adds a violation. Continue until the glass is almost overflowing.

> *"Before you know it, your glass is filled. A person with a glass filled with beans is filled with hurt and fear. They may experience this state of being with ongoing depression, rage, sickness, lack of energy, loss of self-worth, or little hope for the future. Since it is our birthright to be an empty glass—to be filled with light, joy, worth, passion, peace, and love—and few of us want to live in pain, whether that the pain is in our body or shows up in the mental and emotional burden of fear, stress, anger, and sadness, we try to find ways to empty our cups."*

> *"We seek out ways to empty our glass—things like Facebook, television, shopping, or drugs and alcohol—but those do not take away our beans. They are only distractions that temporarily take away our focus from our glass of wounds. And so, they offer only a temporary sense of relief, but generally in the long term, take away our valuable energy and time."*

✳ Take several beans from the bowl and add them to the glass.

> *"We know love can have the ability to heal our wounds, so often we turn to other people to empty our glasses. But people who are wounded often inadvertently pass on their beans to the other. So ultimately, when we're seeking love from a wounded place or from another who is wounded, we are often receiving or adding beans (and wounds) in the process."*

✳ To illustrate this, put down the two glasses (which should be full of beans). Take a handful of beans from each cup and then pour the beans from each hand into the opposite glass.

> *"So the big question is how can we empty our glass of beans?"*

✳ Allow participants to respond and discuss. The discussion should touch on what fulfills them, among other things.

> *"Now let's say we were to empty our glasses."*

✳ Empty the beans from a glass.

> *"What if I were to drop this glass and it shattered? What would become of you?*
>
> *Are you the glass or was the glass only a symbolic container?"*

GROUP DISCUSSION

- How would you describe the feeling of wholeness?
- Do you believe every person has the ability, at any moment, to be whole?
- What keeps you from experiencing this sense of wholeness?

PARENT PATH

Place a bowl of beans and one or several glasses (each glass designated to a family member) somewhere in the house. Family members can fill their cup with beans signifying their emotional state. In this way, family members have a simple way to identify and communicate their emotional state without having to engage verbally. This can be especially useful with teenagers who least want to explain their feelings when they are upset.

HERE AND NOW

"Drink your tea slowly and reverently, as if it is the axis on which the world earth revolves—slowly, evenly, without rushing toward the future; live the actual moment. Only this moment is life."

—THICH NHAT HANH

INSPIRATION

Mindfulness is not only a practice; it is a state of being. It is the ability to focus our attention and establish a presence of mind that enables us to open our heart so that we are better able to authentically connect with something—be it a person, place, object, or moment. From this open and present state, we become channels for all the possibility that the present holds.

MUSICAL SELECTION

Vienna Teng, "Feather Moon"

MATERIALS

Musical selection (choose your own) and stereo

Fruit (strawberries and grapes are ideal)

Sticky easel pad 25"x 30"

Four felt pens

Participants' journals

INSTRUCTIONS

* Discuss with the group the concept of mindfulness and have participants share one activity or moment that they were fully engaged and present for.

* Participants will take part in four exercises with the intention of activating their senses and practicing mindful awareness. After each exercise, participants will write down in their journal one or two descriptive words that best conveys the essence (quality or characteristic) of what they tasted, heard, saw, or felt.

✳ **Taste** Distribute a piece of fruit to every participant. Before and while participants put the piece of fruit in their mouth, ask them to be aware of the following points:

> **Look at the fruit. What is your mouth doing in anticipation of putting the fruit in your mouth?**
>
> **Have participants begin eating the fruit, chewing *slowly* and *thoroughly*. Have them focus on textures and the flavor(s) that exist when the fruit first enters their mouth, and then what the flavor and texture does over time in their mouth.**

After they have finished eating the piece of fruit, have participants write in their journal a descriptive word or two that best captures the essence of what they tasted.

✳ **Hear** Have participants sit comfortably and close their eyes. Begin playing the musical selection. Remind participants to keep their attention on the music and notice:

> **What instruments they can identify**
>
> **The rise and fall of melodies**
>
> **The lyrics (if applicable)**
>
> **Any emotions that come up for them while listening**

When the piece is over, have participants write in their journal a word or two that best captures the essence of what they heard.

✳ **Sight** Have participants get in dyads (with someone they don't usually partner with) and have them sit directly across from one another. Have partners look into each other's eyes. When they begin, mention that it is normal to feel self-conscious from someone staring at them so intently. Advise them to remain totally silent and try to push through the initial feeling of self-consciousness, and instead direct their attention to the features of *their* partner's eyes:

> **Colors**
>
> **Shape**
>
> **Light**
>
> **Any emotions that they may be able to decipher through the eyes**

HERE AND NOW

The facilitator should time partners' looking into each other's eyes for about one minute. Once the time has passed, have participants write in their journal the word or two that best captures the essence of what they saw.

* **Feel** Clear a large space in the room. Have participants spread out from one another and then close their eyes. Begin playing the musical selection and ask them to begin by just listening to the music and allow it to enter their bodies. Allow thirty seconds to go by. Ask participants to notice where they feel the music in their body, and what their body is wanting to do. Encourage participants, if they feel inclined, to begin moving their body in accordance to what their body wants to do (advise participants to stay somewhat within their space so that they don't accidently bump into another participant). Remind participants that if they begin to feel self-conscious, they can stand still, close their eyes and return their focus to the music and how that feels in their body.

  When the piece is over, have participants open their eyes and write in their journal the word or two that best captures the essence of what they felt.

* Write each of the following prompts on a separate sheet of easel paper at the top of the sheet. Place sheets nearby on a wall or other hard surface. Include a felt pen near each sheet:

  Here and now I taste . . .

  Here and now I see . . .

  Here and now I hear . . .

  Here and now I feel . . .

* Ask the girls to write in their journals a poetic sentence to complete the prompts listed above. Each sentence should contain the word(s) that they identified for each of the senses.

  For example: if they wrote down the word "hazel" and "deep," for the sight exercise, then they may write, "Here and now I see hazel wells that dig deep and echo her story."

* Once participants have fashioned their four sentences, ask them to write their sentences (leaving out the "Here and now" portion of the sentence) under each prompt. Make sure you have additional blank easel sheets for extra writing space.

* Finally, read the collective poem out loud to the participants and follow up with a brief discussion.

HERE AND NOW

GROUP DISCUSSION

- What do you notice about the thing you're focusing on when you're fully present?
- What do you notice about yourself when you're fully present?
- What keeps you from being fully present?
- What simple things could you do each day to become more mindful?

PARENT PATH

Since I was young, my mother and I have gone on walks together. Whether it was down to the beach or running errands, she would always stop and have me look at a beautiful window display or cloud formations, or the wings on a perched butterfly. During my teenage years this was annoying to me. But I also remember during those years thinking she was pretty amazing for always noticing lovely, poignant things that other people just walked right by.

To this day, my experience of the world is a little more magical because she taught me to pay attention and really take in the beauty of the world around me. Especially in this day and age when family togetherness sometimes consists of hasty interactions bridged by the Internet, it may be important to practice putting down, as much as possible, our technology and rushed meanderings, and to take notice. Treat your excursions with your daughter like a living museum. Pay attention to light and color in nature, pay attention to interesting human interactions, pay attention to the poetic movement of things coming and going. Your teenage daughter will undoubtedly get annoyed at moments, but you are teaching her something essential about life—that when you pay attention to beauty, or anything for that matter, it will rise up and meet you.

HERE AND NOW

NATURAL MYSTIC

"We are the flow, we are the web.
We are the weavers, we are the web."
—SHEKINAH MOUNTAINWATER

INSPIRATION

According to the Lakota people, the natural world is an extension of the larger fabric that we are all sourced from. The Lakota salutation *Mitakuye Oyasin*, translated as, "To all my relations," is not just a ceremonial acknowledgment. The trees, rock, mountains, sky, river—all are considered family. These elements are living entities that hold consciousness and memory and, with breathtaking generosity, provide all the natural resources humans need to survive and thrive. This is a far different philosophy from the exploitive relationship that many "developed nations" have with nature. Instead the Lakota perspective holds the natural world with reverence and humility and sees the sacred web that binds all things together.

MUSICAL SELECTION

India Arie, "Beautiful"

PREPARATION

If possible, take the group to a natural setting where they can be exposed to many
    different elements of nature in solitude. If this is not possible, try to find a space
    outside with as much privacy and as many natural elements as possible.
Have participants bring their journal and something to write with.
Select a poem(s) about the nature. Suggested: poems by Mary Oliver: "Morning
    Poem," "Wild Geese," "How I Go into the Woods."

INSTRUCTIONS

✳ Once the group has convened and gotten settled, read one of your favorite
    poems about nature. If you have a special love for and relationship with the natu-
    ral world, talk about it as well with the group.

✷ Next, invite the participants to look around them, noticing the earth, the plants and trees, rocks, sky, wind, and any other natural features that they are able to see or sense.

✷ Ask participants to choose one element in nature around them and go sit in a place that allows them to commune with that natural element. Make sure they don't wander too far out of hearing range. Have them bring their journals.

NATURAL MYSTIC

✳ Let participants know that you will facilitate a guided process for them to follow. Remind participants to stay as present as they possibly can for the next several minutes. Give the group a minute to get centered, and then begin reading the sample narration below. Every time an ellipsis (. . .) appears, allow at least a minute for participants to engage with that prompt in the narrative.

> *Take a look at the element you selected. Begin to imagine this element's journey. Imagine the journey it went through to be in front of you right now. Imagine its origin and then try to imagine its entire evolution to its state in the present . . .*
>
> *Begin to notice the physical features of this element: Look at complexity of colors. . . . Look at its texture. Notice how it moves, or take in its stillness. Notice all the little features you might not see if you weren't paying attention . . .*
>
> *Penetrate this element further. What qualities does it hold? Is it playful, wise, strong, forgiving? What about its character can teach you something about yourself or about life in general?*
>
> *Imagine that this element is a living being that can communicate. Open your heart and imagine what message it may be communicating to you . . .*
>
> *Close your eyes. From your heart center, open yourself to this element, and imagine that the boundary between you and this element begins to dissolve. Begin to enter the natural world not as a person from a particular gender, race, or history, or as an outsider looking at nature, but rather as a part of it. Take in what it feels like to let go of your sense of being one, and experience being the whole . . .*
>
> *Slowly bring participants' awareness back to their body, and when they are ready slowly open their eyes.*

✳ Have participants write down whatever they wish in connection to their encounter with their selected natural element. This may be writing thoughts and feelings through stream of consciousness or they might be inspired to write a poem or even draw something. Give participants at least fifteen to twenty minutes to write.

NATURAL MYSTIC

GROUP DISCUSSION

✳ Have participants reconvene in a seated circle. Once seated, participants may share what they wrote in their journals or talk about any thoughts and feelings that came up for them while participating in this activity.

✳ At the end of the share, go around the circle and ask the participants to thank the natural element they focused on for a particular quality. For example: "Thank you, rock, for your grounded presence and teaching me about stillness."

PARENT PATH

Some teenagers have a hard time engaging with the natural world; you can help bridge this divide by taking your daughter on a walk in nature and setting up a scavenger hunt. Create a list of things to discover during your walk together. Below is a list of prompts, but you may make up your own. The prompts are there to foster mindfulness and appreciation; as you begin identifying things in nature, you can check them off the list. Be sure to practice respect for nature and not to remove anything from its place.

Identify something that represents the elements of earth, fire, water, and air.

Identify five sounds in nature.

Identify something in nature that provides either shelter or food to at least three different species.

Identify one thing in nature that contains at least five different colors.

Identify three things in nature without which humans could not survive very long.

Find something that represents you in nature and explain the connection.

BEING GRATEFUL

"Sometimes I need only to stand wherever I am to be blessed."
—MARY OLIVER

INSPIRATION

Recent studies on gratitude, like the Harvard study referenced below, have begun to reveal that it can be a remedy for everything from depression to heart disease. Acknowledging what one is grateful for and feeling grateful are two connected, yet different activities. Giving gratitude can imply that a person is acknowledging something that brings benefit to her life. One can also *experience* gratitude: ushering a felt sense of appreciation, humility, awe, wholeness, and connection. Gratitude is an awareness that allows us to fully feel and identify the love that surrounds us. Even in the most tragic of circumstances, gratitude can be accessed. Through the lens of gratitude, we can view our challenges as learning experiences that break us open and make us wiser and stronger versions of ourselves.

MUSICAL SELECTION

Meshell Ndegeocello, "Thankful"

MATERIALS

Participants' journals

INSTRUCTIONS

✳ Discuss with the group the concepts presented in the Inspiration above.

  Research and present data on benefits of gratitude:

  Emmons and McCullough, "Counting Blessings Versus Burdens," *Journal of Personality and Social Psychology* 2003, Volume 84, No 2, 377–389.

  (http://greatergood.berkeley.edu/pdfs/GratitudePDFs/6Emmons-BlessingsBurdens.pdf;).

  "In Praise of Gratitude." *Harvard Mental Health Letter*, November 1, 2011. (http://www.health.harvard.edu/newsletter_article/in-praise-of-gratitude).

  Ask for participants' ideas about the connection and contrast between giving gratitude and feeling gratitude.

✳ The facilitator, followed by participants, can then describe a time in their life when something very challenging happened to them or a loved one. Talk about, in retrospect, what positive things came forward out of the experience. For example: a deepening of a relationship; positive qualities, such as strength, courage, or compassion, that enlarged their sense of themselves, or taught them something they deeply needed to learn about themselves or about life in general.

✳ Have participants get their journals and write all the things they are grateful for.

✳ After everyone has finished writing their gratitude list, ask participants to connect their written acknowledgment with the feeling sense of appreciation. Have them get comfortable and turn inward. You may read them the following and/or add your own narration.

> *The world is filled with abundance and love that is always available to you. You can access this love and support through gratitude. Feel your heart open and receive that love that surrounds you. Begin by acknowledging the simple and awesome fact that you are alive here and now. Thousands of lives came before you, weaved through their own challenges and triumphs. Many individuals that normally would never have met, serendipitously came together to finally create you. How special you are! You are a being that gets to participate in life here and now: to witness its beauty, to experience its highs and lows, to learn and grow from it, and to create your own song within it. Take in for a moment what it really means to be alive . . .*
>
> *Now focus your gratitude on your body and your health. How wonderful it is to be able to fully use your body, to feel free of pain most of the time. How the body repairs itself and allows you to move in this world with ease and power. And for those of us who have experienced some physical or mental and emotional challenges or illness: What have you learned about yourself through these challenges? Did you discover you are fragile, strong, courageous? What gift did this physical, mental, or emotional challenge bring forward in you or show you about the love that surrounds you; who or what did you learn to appreciate? Take this all in and feel gratitude for the health that you do experience . . .*

BEING GRATEFUL

Finally, focus on some of the things you wrote on your gratitude list. Really open your heart and feel the gift you have been given through the people, opportunities, and material abundance you experience in your life. These gifts are small examples of the even bigger love that surrounds you ...

As an additional option:

✷ You may provide six-inch strings and small tags (with a hole in each) and have participants write on the tags what they are grateful for. They can then tie the tags to a small, designated tree or bush or any other appropriate object. This process can be incorporated every time the group meets or designated as a one-time activity.

✷ After allowing time for the above exercise, have participants gather together in a circle and take turns talking about the things they are grateful for.

GROUP DISCUSSION

- What do you feel and experience when you put your attention on what you appreciate in your life?

- How often do you take time out to focus your attention on what you are grateful for?

- Why might gratitude be something you would want to incorporate into your everyday life?

- If you decide not to do the gratitude tree activity, list the things you are grateful for.

PARENT PATH ....

Incorporating a daily gratitude practice is a simple and powerful way to keep your daughter grounded and positive. These practices can be done while waking her up in the morning, saying good night, or before a meal. In any case, slowing down and turning her attention toward something she is grateful for that day keeps her attention on what is good and right in her world and all the abundance of love and support that surrounds her.

BEING GRATEFUL

READING CROW

"Only the symbolic life can express the need of the soul."
—CARL JUNG

INSPIRATION

The concept of receiving guidance and prophecy through the use of reading symbols or receiving a sign is age old: from the Egyptian mystery schools and Greek oracular culture to the Christian mystics and the shamanistic practices of the Americas. The concept and practice of reading signs historically has suggested 1) some creative intelligence is at play, whether it is our own psyche or a higher intelligence that is communicating to us, and 2) information is being communicated to us through the use of symbols and symbolic interaction in our environment. While some of these cultures relied on messages for prophetic purposes, perhaps we can use this practice as a way of looking at our world in a more down-to-earth context.

Here's an example: One day I was sitting in my office prepared to write, but for the second consecutive day I was struggling with how to convey a complex idea and was completely stuck in the mud. As I looked out my window I saw a man planting a new tree. At the time, he was tilling the soil, reworking the dirt so that it would loosen up and provide more oxygen to the tree's roots. When he finished, a crow landed on a No Parking sign just in front of my window. At that moment, I felt like there was something in that scene before me that was important—a sign that both reflected my struggle and illuminated the solution.

At the time, I didn't know entirely what to make of this scene, but later that day I interpreted what felt like a truth: The man tilling the soil could represent moving ideas and words around and letting them breathe, so that I don't get too set on how a particular concept may get expressed. The crow is a bird, often symbolic of a messenger. Its color, black, sometimes represents mystery and magic. And it so happened that this crow landed on the No Parking sign—a message cautioning against immobility. Later that day, as it turned out, after pondering the narrative several times over, I took a break from writing and gave myself some breathing space. An hour later a strange and unorthodox idea landed in my consciousness that allowed me to move out of my immobility and finish writing.

Clearly these "signs" could be read in hundreds of different ways. That is the beauty of symbolic language: there is no wrong or right way of interpreting; you see what you are able and need to see. Whether this symbolic sight is our own invention devised to make meaning of our environment or cryptic messages to us from beyond, I do not know. But reading our environment in this manner creates magic and lends wisdom to our world.

MUSICAL SELECTION

Imani Uzuri, "Sun Moon Child"

MATERIALS

Participant journals

A book or website of symbols interpretation. References with cross-cultural
    interpretations—multiple interpretations from different cultures—is ideal.

PREPARATION

As the facilitator, think about your own stories pertaining to a sign, like the one in the introduction, that you could share with the group. Or, conduct this exercise prior to meeting with the group so that you can talk about your experience of the activity.

INSTRUCTIONS

✳ Discuss the following:

> The belief and practice of many cultures throughout time of interpreting their environment through dreams, visions, the weather and even animals, to receive understanding and guidance from more universal forces.

> Reading signs means interpreting the significance of such phenomena as visions, dreams, natural objects and occurences. For instance, a shaman or priest interprets visions and signs for a person or community seeking understanding. In more modern, secularized examples, the symbolic world, such as that of dreams, may be interpreted through a specialized psychologist or even through reference material on symbols. In either case the information is generally fixed and sourced by someone or something outside the person seeking understanding.

> Come up with an example of a symbol; for example, a snake. Ask participants to make guesses on what they think a snake means symbolically. Then refer to a book or website on symbols and read to the group the interpretations

READING CROW

presented there. Talk about any commonalities or differences across different cultures on the given symbol.

Now talk about how symbols can also be interpreted from a more personal source, through one's own personal associations and experiences. For example, a person at a particular moment may be feeling very lonely and anxious and then suddenly a black cat crosses their path. Rather than interpreting the black cat based on the collective perception of bad luck, this person may be reminded of their deceased grandmother's black cat, who provided great comfort and love. Therefore, this sign could provide this person a felt sense of connection and comfort.

Have participants write and/or share any personal associations and experiences they have had with snakes (or another suggested symbol). For example: what they learned about them growing up, a personal experience, or a friend or a family member they may associate with that symbol. Have them compare their personal experiences with the referenced interpretations of the symbol.

Share with the group a personal story about an incident in which you read your environment as a sign or message and what it meant.

Next, have participants share any of their own experiences that might illustrate their own encounters with "signs," or looking at objects and events symbolically.

✳ Ask participants to think about something in their life around which they need clarity: a difficult situation or conflict, a big transition, or a decision they need to make. Ask them to write about it in their journal.

✳ Instruct participants, before you reconvene as a group, to look for a sign(s) in their daily environment that may illuminate an issue or decision on which they need guidance. They may look to the natural world, animals, music, signposts, dreams, interactions they have with others, and so on. Participants may not fully understand at that moment why something seems significant, but it is important that when they experience a moment drawing them in, as if time is slowing down and something special is being communicated to them, that they take notice.

✳ Follow up at the next session and ask participants to share their experiences.

READING CROW

PARENT PATH ....

In the Jungian psychoanalytic perspective, dreams are believed to be the symbolic conversation between the unconscious and conscious minds. Many cultures believe dreams communicate vital and even prophetic information regarding individual and collective states of being.

You may encourage your daughter to honor her dreams by keeping a dream journal by her bed and recording her dreams. This works best if your daughter does it as soon as she wakes up—before talking, brushing her teeth, checking her phone, or even getting out of bed. In addition, ask your daughter about her dreams and, if she's interested, tell her yours. This is an opportunity to connect at a time when she may be hesitant to share details of her daily waking life.

THE VOICE WITHIN

> **"I have been a seeker and still am but I stopped asking the books
> and the stars. I started listening to the teaching of my soul."**
> **—RUMI**

INSPIRATION

Associative memory is the basis of our thought process. Through our basic senses and memory we process information and make deductions and decisions, based essentially on our past. Some of these interpretations and decisions prove to be right and some do not. There is, however, another executive thinking function: intuition. Less is known about intuition. Intuition can be a kind of "sixth sense" that can sometimes provide uncanny wisdom (in the form of a thought, feeling, or even an image). The more we call upon and honor our intuition, the more access we have to its wisdom, and the more we can direct our lives from this source.

MUSICAL SELECTION

Kate Bush, "This Woman's Work"

MATERIALS

Journals

INSTRUCTIONS

✳ Discuss the concept of intuition with the group. You may draw on your own understanding of and experiences with your own intuition.

✳ Next, have participants get into pairs facing each other. Have one participant be the listener and the other the speaker. Allow the speakers five minutes to explain an issue or decision they need some clarity around. They can include whatever information they would like to reveal about the situation.

✳ The listener will remain silent and not ask about or comment on any part of her partner's narrative. After the five minutes is up, have all the listeners turn within, closing their eyes and focusing on the area in the middle of their chest. Instruct them to ask from this place for a response to their partner's issue. Remind them not to force anything, but just to allow information to come forward naturally. If they feel their attention shift to their head and notice they are trying to work out the "best" response in their head, ask them to gently shift their attention back to their heart center. Responses may take the form of feelings, images, or even a word or phrase. Tell them it is important not to censor or ignore what comes up, and allow them to take as much time as needed. When they feel they have a response, ask them to open their eyes.

✳ The listener can share the response they received. The speaker can talk about their own associations and possible interpretations of the listener's response.

✳ Partners then will shift roles and do the exercise again.

✳ An additional option is to have participants write down for one week any moments when they had an intuitive feeling about something facing them, and what, if anything, was the outcome. Have them share those moments at the next session.

GROUP DISCUSSION

- **How do you experience your inner voice? Through words, feelings, images?**
- **Do you trust your own intuitive wisdom?**
- **How do you know when you are receiving intuitive wisdom versus just listening to fear or logic?**
- **Has there been a time in which you have heard your own intuitive wisdom and didn't follow it? What happened?**
- **What stops you from following through on your intuition?**

THE VOICE WITHIN

PARENT PATH

The tendency for children to use their parents as both sounding board and counsel generally dims during adolescence. As a result, your daughter's ability to access her own internal guidance systems is crucial. Introduce this exercise to your daughter when she needs to make a hard decision or is battling a situation that appears to be undermining her sense of stability. In addition, if your daughter is open to it, The Voice Within exercise can be used in an alternative way: when you and your daughter are at an impasse as a result of a conflict, set up two chairs and allow each of you to articulate your argument to the other. Then change chairs, and change roles. You will articulate your daughter's perspective, feelings, and needs, and she will articulate yours. Both parties will then switch chairs one last time and employ the centering process described above, directing their attention to finding resolution—however that may reveal itself. Express to one another what words, images, or feelings came forward.

THE LOVE OF THOUSANDS, PART I

"Walking, I am listening to a deeper way.
Suddenly all my ancestors are behind me. Be still, they say.
Watch and listen. You are the result of the love of thousands."
—LINDA HOGAN

INSPIRATION

We all have ancestors: family lineages dating back to the beginning of time, whose stories we carry in our DNA. It is because of the work and sacrifice of our ancestors that we are bestowed with some of the blessings that we possess today—both materially and spiritually. And where they fell short, it is up to us to pick up the thread and follow through on what they could not. We keep the spirit of our ancestors' legacy alive when we acknowledge their existence and contributions, and fulfill our own life's purpose and potential.

MUSICAL SELECTION

Chevela Vargas, "La Llorona"

MATERIALS

Tape

Copies of Ancestry Tree worksheet for each participant

PREPARATION

Before this session, hand out the Ancestry Tree worksheet (see next page). Ask participants to conduct research on their ancestry. Have them interview their parent(s) and, if possible, grandparents to discover names, racial, and ethnic origins and any significant stories or interesting facts associated with deceased family members. In the case that participants are not in contact with both of their biological parents, they may choose to focus on information involving their racial or ethnic background.

Remind participants to fill out the Ancestry Tree worksheet to the best of their ability. Participants may use the worksheet provided or come up with their own graphic depiction of their ancestry tree. Participants should include all known names

Ancestry Tree worksheet

of their family lineage in the diagram. In addition, they may write an identifying word next to the name to cue the participant about a particular story or interesting fact concerning that ancestor.

Facilitator: Draw your own ancestry tree as described above before this session. You will use this as a visual aid for participants to reference before they map out their own.

INSTRUCTIONS

✳ Discuss the significance of ancestry.

- **Read the selected quote to participants and ask them for their thoughts.**
- **What is your understanding of an ancestor?**
- **What is the significance, if any, of ancestors in our lives today?**

At the following session when participants have completed their ancestral tree:

✳ Each participant will introduce the oral history of her ancestry to the group, including any stories or facts about particular ancestors she would like to share with the group. She may choose to tape her ancestral diagram to a wall or hard surface for others to see.

✳ Follow up by asking every group member, after they have shared, to talk about the significance of learning about their ancestry.

THE LOVE OF THOUSANDS

THE LOVE OF THOUSANDS

PARENT PATH

One of the most powerful and relevant projects you can do with your daughter is uncovering her family lineage. Collect stories, pictures, and small artifacts of her ancestry. You may also want to use online sources like ancestory.com or even visit a Mormon church, which often has extensive background information. When you have completed your search, gather everything and develop an art project together based on what you collected. Below are a few examples of creative projects:

Create a family tree like that described in the activity above. Embellish the diagram with photos, color, background imagery, and small symbolic objects.

Create a beautiful ancestor altar in your home. Include photos, candles, flowers, artifacts, and objects symbolic of an ancestor's ethnicity, profession, gifts, etc.

Create a video montage with music and old photos of the family lineage in chronological order ending with your daughter (and her siblings).

Copy pictures or photos of your daughter's ancestors. Embellish the photocopies creatively with color, glitter, and/or imagery surrounding the photo. Glue the final product on a seven-day candle (candles sold for about $2.00 at large drugstores and some grocery stores that are about a foot high and contained in glass).

THE LOVE OF THOUSANDS, PART II: ANCESTOR BRACELETS

GROUP DISCUSSION

- In what ways do we carry our ancestors with us?
- Is it important for you personally to honor your ancestors? Explain.
- What are different ways of honoring one's ancestors?

MATERIALS

Cording or thread 14 m width or less, of various colors. Each participant will get a yard of each of three colors they select. Cut enough cording of each color beforehand so that participants may each get at least one cord of any color they select.

Gold seed beads (enough for everyone to have at least 20–30 beads)

Crafting or glass beads (one for each participant) with a big enough hole for cording

Safety pins—enough for each participant

One pair of scissors

PREPARATION

Cut all cording into one-yard strands.

Create stations for each of the materials provided.

INSTRUCTIONS

✶ Ask participants to select three colors for their bracelet. Have them think about colors that they want to represent their racial or ethnic background.

✶ Next, have them gather at least twenty gold seed beads. These beads represent their ancestors. Have them also select one glass bead. This bead will represent themselves. Lastly, distribute safety pins.

✶ Have participants line up the cords. Take the top three inches of the cords and make a small loop about the size of the circumference of their glass bead. Have them tie two knots to secure the loop in place.

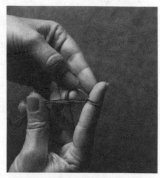

✶ Safety pin the knot to participants clothes or another stable surface.

✶ Start braiding the strands of cord or thread. After about one inch, braid in the gold beads. To begin, thread a bead onto the outer left strand. Push the bead against the base of the braid, and cross the left strand over the middle. Now have them thread another bead onto the outer right strand. Push the bead to the base of the braid and cross over. Repeat until they have used all the gold beads.

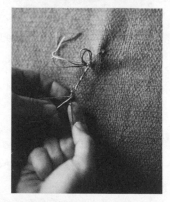

✶ Have participants braid any remaining strands until it measures perfectly around the wrist; then tie two or three knots to secure braiding.

✶ Finally, thread in the glass bead through the remaining strings and knot cording following the bead with two or three knots. Cut any remaining strings after the last knots.

SPIRITUAL MOSAIC

**"People take different roads seeking fulfillment and happiness.
Just because they're not your road does not mean they are lost."**
—DALAI LAMA

INSPIRATION

Joseph Campbell, a mythology scholar and author, once wrote, "The truth is one; the sages call it by many names." The quote references an idea that there exist countless names, philosophies, and practices to address a transcendent principle. One of the great basic freedoms of our modern era is to be able to choose, or not have to choose, a philosophy that resonates with our own concept of transcendence.

MUSICAL SELECTION

Meshell Ndegeocello, "Fellowship"

MATERIALS

Paper and pens

PREPARATION

On small pieces of paper, write/type the words or phrases that depict a particular spiritual concept or tool. There should be enough concepts to match the number of participants. Below are some examples, but you may add or create your own.

Karma	Satori
Reincarnation	Orishas
Hijab	Archetypes
Yoga	The Five Pillars
Teshuva	Four Noble Truths
Medicine Wheel	Chakras
Samsara	Walking the Red Road
Myth of Sophia/Gnosis	Anima/Animus
Tikkun Olam	The Singularity

INSTRUCTIONS

* Fold small pieces of paper and put them into a bowl. Have participants select one.

* Participants will research their concept at home and put together a presentation that should not exceed five minutes. The presentation should include at least the following:

    Which religious or spiritual tradition, if any, the concept comes from

    A description of the concept

    Any other relevant information that would help the group to understand the concept further

    Something that embodies the concept they chose. They may present a song, painting, poem, or a part of a film—anything that depicts the essence of the concept

* After each presentation, group members may ask questions of the participant regarding the concept they presented.

GROUP DISCUSSION

• **Was there a particular concept presented that really resonated for you? Evoked curiosity? Evoked resistance or disbelief?**

• **Did you notice any parallels in the different concepts presented?**

• **Do you think you need to be a part of a particular religion or spiritual tradition to be a spiritual person? Explain.**

• **What is spirituality to you?**

SPIRITUAL MOSAIC

PARENT PATH ....

For parents that come from a particular religious affiliation, one of the most challenging issues is relinquishing control of their adolescent's spiritual affiliation. Finding one's spiritual home is an incredibly personal endeavor. When a young person genuinely connects with a transcendent moment and/or philosophy it can be the foundation of their resilience, morality, and inner peace. However, when religion or spiritual philosophy is forced upon a young person, it may not offer the same benefits that a genuine, personal connection bestows.

Most parents want what's best for their children. As an adult, you may have found solace, connection, and, in some cases, even salvation through your spiritual practice. As a parent you undoubtedly want the same for your child; but by adolescence, your child has the prerogative to explore and decide what truly satiates her soul. Every healthy and genuine relationship, be it a personal bond or a spiritual association, should be engaged in from a position of freedom and self-determination. Kahlil Gibran wrote most eloquently on this point:

Your children are not your children.

They are the sons and daughters of Life's longing for itself.

They come through you, but not from you,

And though they are with you, yet they belong not to you.

You may give them your love but not your thoughts,

For they have their own thoughts.

You may house their bodies but not their souls,

For their souls dwell in the house of tomorrow,

Which you cannot visit, not even in your dreams.

You may strive to be like them

But seek not to make them like you.

For life goes not backward nor tarries with yesterday . . .

SPIRITUAL MOSAIC

THE BIG QUESTIONS*

> "Be patient toward all that is unsolved in your heart and try
> to love the questions themselves, like locked rooms and like books
> that are now written in a very foreign tongue. Do not now seek the answers,
> which cannot be given you because you would not be able to live them.
> And the point is, to live everything. Live the questions now. Perhaps you will then
> gradually, without noticing it, live along some distant day into the answer."
> —RAINER MARIA RILKE

INSPIRATION

In my experience, adolescents' desire to probe the existential world is insatiable. Not only are their questions big, but the responses they are met with are often complex and contradictory. In asking these questions and receiving a multitude of responses, young people begin to understand that the world is both mysterious and multifaceted—and this discovery alone invigorates their search for their own truth and purpose.

MUSICAL SELECTION

Joan Osborne, "One of Us"

PREPARATION

✳ Ask participants to brainstorm the "big" questions about life that they are curious about. For example:

- Why are we here? What is the purpose of life?
- What happens after we die?
- Why do bad things happen to good people?
- Why do bad people who cause great harm to others sometimes seem to live their entire lives without being brought to "justice" for what they did?
- Do you believe in a higher power, and, if so, how would you describe it?
- What do you think is the fate of humans?
- What is the significance of dreams?
- If love is supposed to be such a beautiful thing, why does it sometimes hurt so much?

✳ Record participants' questions on an easel board. If some questions come up that seem redundant, write them next to the questions they seem to mirror.

✳ After the brainstorm, write the core questions, omitting redundancies, on small strips of paper.

✳ Fold the pieces of paper so participants can't see their contents and put the papers in some kind of container. Have each participant select one.

✳ After each participant has picked a question, they will seek out, within the following week, at least five people to respond to the question they selected. They may record the responses on video or audio recorder (on most smartphones) or write them down. Participants should ask people from many different walks of life (different ages, races and ethnicities, education, spiritual beliefs, etc.). *Responses should be no longer than one minute.* Make sure the participants indicate the time limit before the person interviewed responds.

✳ Have participants choose the best three to five responses (those responses that are the most thought-out and are unique from other responses) to share at the next session.

INSTRUCTIONS (May be broken into two different sessions)

✳ Have participants sit in a circle or around a table.

✳ Have each participant share the question she asked the respondents and then share the three to five responses that she selected.

✳ Group members are asked to just listen to the responses without comments or extraneous reactions.

✳ Next, participants will be asked to respond themselves to the questions posed above. (This may be during the same session or designated for another session.) Before they begin responding, go over the basic guidelines outlined in Group Discussions in the Getting Started section located at the beginning of this guide.

✳ As the facilitator, you may ask questions to help a participant clarify an idea, but be mindful not to insert any of your personal philosophy or beliefs into this group discussion.

THE BIG QUESTIONS

GROUP DISCUSSION

- If we can't prove something, does that make it less real? Explain.

- Do you think it is essential that everyone has answers to these big questions in life? Why or why not?

- After hearing so many different responses to these questions, what can we say about "the truth"?

- Acknowledge participants' wisdom and (if true) their ability to hold different truths without making anyone wrong.

PARENT PATH ....

The same kind of existential questioning in the group exercise can be applied at home (a good catalyst of discussion is a documentary called *The Big Questions*). Come up with a list of questions. Remind everyone that no one, regardless of age or education, holds the absolute truth regarding these questions, and each family member should try to hold others' ideas with openness and respect. This family exercise is ideal because it promotes abstract thinking, and if done in the spirit of openness, is also a discussion that equalizes ideas and opinions between parent and child. This provides your daughter an opportunity to explore and express her ideas without being invalidated by.

* Modified from an exercise by Rachel Kessler.

SACRED BOX

"Love's greatest gift is its ability to make everything it touches sacred."
—BARBARA DE ANGELIS

INSPIRATION

The term sacred is generally given to something—a person, place, or object—held in reverence and awe. The word comes from the Latin word *sacer*, meaning set aside. The author and cultural anthropologist Mircea Eliade wrote in his book *The Sacred and the Profane* that the sacred always manifests itself as a reality different from secular reality; it may fit into the context of this world but has a quality to it that is otherworldly. It is often presumed that when something sacred manifests itself to the beholder, that person is blessed to be a witness to something rare and divine. I believe that when any of us are aware of something with significant presence and openness, we create a quality of sacredness, allowing us to live in a world where the sacred is ever-present.

MUSICAL SELECTION

Amel Larrieux, "Sacred"

MATERIALS

Participant journals

Craft papers—various colors and patterns

Blank white paper

Paint—acrylic (at least a twelve-ounce tube of white, black, red, yellow, and
blue paint)

Paintbrushes (five)

Three containers for water (for cleaning paint from brushes)

Magazines and/or old calendars (as many as possible)

Scissors (as many as at least half the number of participants)

Glitter, shells, sequins, or any other craft embellishments

Crafting glue—for at least half the number of participants

Craft box—one for each participant (see: www.store.specialtyschool.com). If you do
not have the budget or time to get craft boxes, you may have participants find a
cigar box, shoebox, or any other box that is no larger than 8"x 3".

INSTRUCTIONS

✳ Have participants write in their journals about what the word and concept
"sacred" means to them. This may include what is most special in their life, a set
of values, depictions of nature, and/or a particular religious or spiritual idea. They
may come up with a formal definition or individual words that embody the concept. Give them at least fifteen minutes to journal, and then ask for participants
who wish to share what they wrote.

✳ Introduce the upcoming activity. Explain that they will symbolize their own
idea of what sacred means to them visually. They will do this by constructing a
Sacred Box.

✳ Present the different boxes they can use and show participants the materials
they will have access to for embellishing their Sacred Box. Play with ideas of different ways participants could work with the materials to create their boxes. The

SACRED BOX

first session could be used to prime their boxes with a base paint or background and to begin to collect images from magazines.

∗ Instruct participants to find small objects, photos or images, quotes and poems that further embody their idea of sacredness. Have them collect all the things in a bag or container and bring it to the following session to incorporate into their box. Allow one or two additional sessions to allow participants to put all the elements together to create their Sacred Box.

∗ After the boxes have been created, give participants some time to write up an artist's statement pertaining to their Sacred Box. They may do this in any written form; for example, they can describe all the elements symbolized in the Sacred Box, write a poem, or write down their own definition of sacred.

∗ When participants have finished, the group can gather and share their Sacred Boxes.

OR

∗ Set up tables around the room and have participants place their Sacred Boxes somewhere on one of the tables along with their artist's statements. Play background music and allow participants to meander around the room on their own and discover each Sacred Box.

6

CLOSING RITUAL

A ritual is a poignant way to connect and bring focus and intention to a moment. In essence, ritual ascribes sacredness to a bond, an event, an idea, an aspiration or vow. At the closure of most rites of passage, the initiates, those participating in the rite, are reunited with their community and are acknowledged, in a ritualistic ceremony, for marking their transition from a child into a newly emerging adult. The closing ritual, also referred to as a reunification ceremony, marks a time of recognition and celebration for both the initiate and her community.

Creating a closing ritual can be a deeply personal and creative process. The ritual should include ideas generated by the group, or ideas of your own making, tailored to your group's participants and their particular identities and experiences. The following guidelines for a closing ritual are only there to offer basic ideas for your own group's closing process.

Once you have sketched out the details of the closing ritual, share this information with the participants. Make sure that they understand the whole flow of the event, as well as the things they need to do and obtain to prepare for the event. Ask participants at least three weeks ahead of the ritual to give you their invite list, and make sure at least one parent, guardian, or other close adult can attend for each participant (and collect their contact information if you don't already have it). Contact the parent(s)/or guardian(s) as soon as possible with the date of the closing ritual, and inform them that they will need to create a Parent Statement (see below) that they will deliver to their daughter at the closing ceremony.

Preparations

THE FACILITATOR

A week or two prior to the closing ritual:

✷ Go over the Closing Ritual worksheet with all participants. Remind girls to make sure they bring with them all the elements in the worksheet, including their ancestors' names, their creative I-statement, and their object of growth, something they have chosen to represent what they want most for themselves in the future.

✷ Think about what you would like to say to begin and end the closing ritual. For the opening of the event, you may want to include:

> **Your intention for starting the group**
>
> **Some of the themes and activities the group explored**
>
> **Moments and qualities of the group that stood out for you**
>
> **The importance of the closing ritual**

✷ Think of and/or write a paragraph about each girl, recognizing what makes her special.

The day of:

✷ Display around the room the various projects that came out of some of the group activities. For example: Boxed In, Beauty Export, Mediacracy, Lighthouses, Here and Now, Sacred Box, etc.

✷ Create a special space for parents and participants to sit. Seating can be arranged with everyone facing in one direction or in a circular or horseshoe fashion, but girls should all be seated together in the first row with their parent(s) or guardian(s) behind them. If possible, place a small table nearby decorated with a beautiful cloth, a candle, and flowers.

✷ Set up some basic refreshments and moving background music, perhaps selecting world music with a female vocalist or soundtrack, or make a playlist from the musical selections suggested in this guide.

CLOSING RITUAL

THE PARTICIPANTS

A week or two prior:

✳ Complete worksheet: Write names of all known ancestors (they can reference the activity "The Love of Thousands"), complete their creative I-statement, and identify their object of growth.

The day of:

✳ Dress in white or, alternatively, in formal attire.

THE PARTICIPANTS' PARENT(S) OR GUARDIAN(S)

A week prior:

✳ Have parent(s)/guardian(s) think about and/or write something addressed to their daughter. Guidelines may include:

Who she was as a young girl

Qualities and talents they see in her today

What they wish for her in the future

✳ Inform parents that they will (verbally) deliver their acknowledgment to their daughters at the closing ceremony. Statements should be about one to three minutes long or one to two pages in length.

Closing Ritual worksheet

1) Ancestor Acknowledgments

My name is _____

My parents are _____

I am the descendant of . . . (List all known ancestors below)

. . . and all my other ancestors whom I do not know, but whose life and legacy have contributed to my existence today.

2) Creative I-Statement   Write a creative statement, poem, video or song that expresses who you are. This is your mythical story, your song, your declaration to the world of your unique presence on this earth.

3) Object of Growth   Think about a quality you want more of in your life that you believe would make you a happier, healthier version of you. For example: patience, discipline, forgiveness, self-love or discernment. Then find an object that represents that quality. Bring the object with you to the closing ritual.

4) Closing Remarks   Think about any closing remarks you would like to say (optional and needs to be no longer then 1 minute).

The Event

WELCOME

✳ Have participants bring their parent(s)/guardian(s) into the space in the ritualistic manner that participants usually use to enter the space, as suggested in the Getting Started section of this book.

✳ Have participants take their parent(s)/guardian(s) around the room and explain the various projects displayed around the room.

✳ Encourage participants to introduce their parent(s)/guardian(s) to other participants and their parent(s)/guardian(s).

✳ Once most parties have arrived and circulated around the room, ask everyone to have a seat.

THE OPENING

✳ The facilitator should introduce herself, welcome the parent(s)/guardian(s), and talk about the group and the importance of a closing ritual.

THE BASIC STRUCTURE

✳ One at a time, participants will stand before the group, introduce themselves, introduce their parent(s)/guardian(s), and then acknowledge their ancestors by reading or reciting their names out loud.

✳ Next, each participant will read or perform their creative I-statement.

✳ Group members, followed by the facilitator, will voice their appreciation for that participant's qualities and gifts, and will make any other acknowledgments they wish to say aloud (1–2 minutes for each participant).

✳ The parent(s)/guardian(s) will address their daughter with the statement they have prepared.

✳ Finally, the participant will bring forward her object of growth, explain its meaning, and place it on a designated table/altar. She may also take time to say any closing remarks (no longer than 2 minutes).

CLOSING RITUAL

CLOSING RITUAL

CLOSING

✷ After each girls has had the opportunity to stand in front of the group, the facilitator should say some final words. You may choose to incorporate a poem or quote and make sure to thank parents and, most important, the participants. You may end the ritual by asking everyone to form a circle. You may incorporate a song or an invocation, or ask everyone present to come up with a word that captures a quality or intention that they would like to invoke for the participants to part with. Alternatively, the group can form a human tunnel (two lines of people facing each other) for initiates to walk through. As each participant walks through, the others whisper a wish for her as she passes. Girls may be blind-folded as they enter the human tunnel and then a designated person can take off the blindfold when they reach the end of the tunnel.

✷ At the end of the ritual, allow time for everyone to socialize. Participants may pick up all their displayed projects and object of growth before they leave.

PARENT PATH ....

Developing a ritual or "growth gathering" for your daughter is a beautiful way to acknowledge her gradual transition into womanhood or any other transition you would like to mark in a meaningful way.

Who is going to be part of the ritual? Most rites of passage, in a traditional context, involve the community. Your daughter's community may include her immediate family, close friends, extended family members, close family friends, teachers, coaches, and mentors with whom she may have an especially close relationship.

You should ask your daughter what people in her community she would like to invite to this gathering. Often, some young women get a little uneasy at the prospect of a parent holding a ritual in front of her friends and family. In that case, you can remind her that you just want to take a brief moment to acknowledge her with a close-knit group of her choosing—those she loves and who love her back.

Where? The beach? Your backyard? A favorite circle of trees? The spot you choose for the gathering may have sentimental value or just be visually beautiful—just make sure it is special.

What to do? Take a look at the format for the closing ritual of the group. This growth ritual would be centered on your daughter, so you will need to alter the process slightly. For example:

Ask each member of the community to come to the gathering with a small object (small enough to put in a satchel) like a pendant, statuette, item from nature, etc., symbolizing one of her qualities or alternatively, a quality they want her to carry into the future. Each person will have a turn to speak and present the object to her. Have people take their time and use anecdotes to illustrate moments when they really got to "see" her and what makes her so special. Provide a beautiful satchel that she can put all the objects in and keep it with her as a memento and reminder.

CLOSING RITUAL

Let your daughter know ahead of time about the gathering and that she will have an opportunity to address the group. She may choose to prepare something, or she may just speak from her heart after everyone has had a chance to share.

You may open and close the gathering in any fashion you choose. There are some suggestions in the group process offered above, as well as in the Getting Started section of this book.

In addition, you may choose to incorporate other ideas into the ritual. The following are just a few suggestions:

Invite your daughter to collect items symbolizing her youth, including a letter to her future self. Place them in a sturdy container as a time capsule and bury it in a special place.

Put together a video slideshow of pictures of your daughter through the years and accompany it with meaningful music.

Incorporate a beautiful poem, like one of those suggested here:

"The Invitation," Oriah Mountain Dreamer

"I Will Not Die an Unlived Life," Dawna Markova

"Our Deepest Fear," Marianne Williamson

"If," Rudyard Kipling

Or show "Today I Rise," a short video available online from WiseatHeart.com

Finally, if possible, have someone capture the gathering on film. The video will be a keepsake from this very special moment in her life and will bring her joy and reflection in the years to come.

CLOSING RITUAL

Conclusion

In 1989, my junior year in high school, I enrolled in a newly-formed elective peer-counseling class. The group of students that showed up for the first day of class was comprised of twelve juniors and seniors of different genders and racial and socioeconomic backgrounds. One by one, we streamed in that first day, defensive and awkward, like a scene from John Hughes's 1985 film classic, *The Breakfast Club*. I remember Mrs. Smith saying at the beginning of the first class that we wouldn't learn how to counsel others until we had "worked on ourselves." Even though Mrs. Smith couldn't have been a day over thirty, and was really hired to teach ninth-grade English, she seemed to know what she was talking about. Something about this work made my heart leap up and scream out "Yes!"

We spent the whole first semester discussing themes ranging from our relationship to our parents to our emerging sexuality. We shared our ideas, personal experiences, songs, and, occasionally, tender and vulnerable moments that seemed so different from the sterile and impersonal academic institution in which I had felt so invisible. The class was my lifeboat at a turbulent time in my life, and, if I were to be honest, one of the only enduring and valuable things I took away from high school. About twelve years later, I helped develop and co-run a program that evolved into an elective class somewhat similar in scope but far more developed, called TryUMF (Trying to Uplift My Folks). This unique program included both social-emotional and radical social theory components and served an average of one hundred students a year from different racial and socioeconomic backgrounds and learning abilities. To this day, students have returned to me, in their twenties, to tell me what a profound impact the class had and how much it shaped their life. They recall their favorite lessons and moving moments in class and say that they could not have made it through high school without it.

These educational and healing experiences that adults can provide for young people are crucial: they are a safe refuge from the onslaught of destructive forces that confront adolescents on a daily basis. They are experiences that allow young people to explore and thrive in a setting where they may have otherwise felt disempowered. They impart social-emotional tools and understanding that the young people will carry with them throughout their lives, and which allow them to see themselves and their world with depth and meaning. These spaces save and transform young people's lives—and those young people grow up ready to enrich the world around them. I can think of very few things that adults can offer young people that are more significant than this.

The youth of every generation inevitably hold the future in their hands. How that future plays out has much to do with the collective character of their generation and where they individually and collectively are directing their energy: Are young people connected to their authentic selves, and do they know how to make decisions from that place? Can they channel their emotional intelligence, compassion, and talent to counter the nihilistic forces, both material and psychic, that threaten what is precious in this world? Do they value the water, the redwoods, and the animals as much as they do their clothes and phones, and do they see a grander vision at play that they can claim to be a part of? Thomas Moore, author of *Care of the Soul: A Guide for Cultivating Depth and Sacredness in Everyday Life,* once wrote, "I can't imagine anything more important to our society than to bring back soul into the education of our youth."[1] If what he meant was to connect our youth with their core essence of themselves, others, and the world around them, then I would have to agree. I believe it will be because of young people's profound experiences with soul that our world will right injustices and endure.

If you work with young people or are raising one, it is not the time in the human life cycle to be passive. While it is true that young people need to find their way into their own truth and existence, there is something inside of them and surrounding them that deserves to be fought for; to be insistent and uncompromising for; to kick and scream from the rooftops of our homes and schools for—something irreplaceable and sacred.

Tell them what they, and this world, mean to you. They will listen. And above all, if we, as adults, are committed to supporting young people in finding their own voices and being heard, we must listen to them.

....

1   John Miller, foreword to *Education and the Soul: Toward a Spiritual Curriculum,* by Thomas Moore (New York: State University of New York Press, 2000), viii.

Additional Resources

RESOURCES FOR FACILITATORS AND PARENTS ON RACE AND IDENTITY

Becoming an Ally: Breaking the Cycle of Oppression. Ann Bishop. (1994) Fernwood: Halifax Productions.

Between Voice and Silence: Women, Girls, Race and Relationship. Jill McLean Taylor, Carol Gilligan, and Amy Sullivan. (1995) Cambridge: Harvard University Press.

The Feminine Mystique. Betty Friedan. (1963). New York: Norton Press.

I Am a Woman: A Native Perspective on Sociology and Feminism. Lee Maracle. (1996) Press Gang.

Sister Outside. Audre Lorde. (1984). New York: Ten Speed Press.

Why Are all The Black Kids Sitting Together in the Cafeteria? Beverly Daniel Tatum. (1997) New York, Basic Books.

RESOURCES FOR PARENTS ON ADOLESCENCE AND PARENTING

The Adolescent Psyche: Jungian and Winnicottian Perspectives. Richard Frankel. (1998). New York: Brunner-Routledge.

Altered Loves: Mothers and Daughters During Adolescence. T. Apter. (1990). New York: Fawcett Columbine.

Get Out of My Life, but First Could You Drive Me and Cheryl to the Mall: A Parent's Guide to the New Teenager. Anthony Wolf. (2002). New York: Farrar, Struas and Giroux.

The Myth of Maturity: What Teenagers Need from Parents to Become Adults. (2001). New York: Norton & Company.

The Price of Privilege: How Parent Pressure and Material Advantage Are Creating a Generation of Disconnected and Unhappy Kids. Madeline Levine. (2008).New York: Harper Collins.

Reviving Ophelia: Saving the Selves of Adolescent Girls. Mary Pipher. (1994). New York: Ballantine Books.

RESOURCES FOR FACILITATORS AND PARENTS ON LGBT, TRANSGENDER, AND DIFFERENTLY-ABLED ISSUES

Transactiveonline.org: Information for parents, professionals, and transgender youth.

Thetrevorproject.org: Crisis intervention for LGBT youth.

This Is a Book for Parents of Gay Kids: A Question + Answer Guide to Everyday Life. Dannielle Owens-Reid and Kristin Russo. (2014). Chronicle Books.

Yodisabledandproud.org: Resources for youth with physical and learning disabilities.

RESOURCES FOR GIRLS

A Young Woman's Survival Guide. (2007). Health Initiatives for Youth. Chico, CA: AK Press.

Colonize This! : Young Women of Color on Today's Feminism. Daisy Hernandez. (2002). Berkeley, CA: Seal Press.

Free Your Mind: The Book for Gay, Lesbian, and Bisexual Youth and Their Allies. Ellen Bass and Kate Kaufman. (1996). New York: Harper Collins.

Girl Power: Young Women Speak Out! Personal Writings from Teenage Girls. Edited by Hillary Carlip. (1995). New York: Warner Books.

What Are You? Voices of Mixed-Race Young People. Pearl Fuyo Gaskins. (1999). New York: Henry Holt.

BLOGS AND ONLINE MAGAZINES

Adiosbarbie.com

Hghw.com (Healthy girls, healthy women)

Itgetsbetter.org (LGBTQ support)

RealColoredGirls.wordpress.com

Redwiremagazine.com

Rookiemag.com

Thickdumplingskin.com

Ywrc.org (Young Women's Resource Center)

In Gratitude to . . .

Rachael Neumann, for your vision and your belief in this work; Jennifer Kamenetz, my editor, for your magic touch, encouragement, and unending patience; Terri Saul, Nancy Fish, Jason Kim, and the entire team at Parallax Press for your work to make it all come to life. Thank you!

Nancy Schiff, Lily Ly, Laurie Lober and Sheilagh Andujar for allowing me the space and trust to carry out my visions without hesitation or barriers.

Dorthy Boswell, my graduate advisor, who saw this work in its seed form and encouraged me to honor it by seeing out its fruition. Rest in Peace and Light.

Darrick Smith, for bringing me into our treasured TryUMF community, in which much of this work was developed. We built an extraordinary container for growth, and I'm so proud of the work we did together.

My sister circle—women whose power, beauty, and passion have touched and influenced me deeply: Kayo, Lillian, Kay, Natalia, Valentina, Michelle, Rena, Imani, Yehnana, Tirien, Juan Won, Shia, Sharon, Amara, Kim and Catherine T.

My Dad and Debbie: Your love and encouragement has meant so much to me. I love you both so much.

My beloved mother: So much of who I am is because of you. Your tremendous belief in me has fueled my own belief in myself. Thank you for your tireless support: your informal edits, your ideas and acting as a sounding board, and most of all for your beautiful, nurturing presence in my life. I love you more than I can express.

Raleigh: I literally could not have done this without you. You are my rock. Your compassion and support has grounded me, your talent inspires me, and your love has transformed me. Thank you for everything you do and are.

To all the hundreds of young people I have worked with in the past and present. You are so extraordinary—each of you is a unique and powerful being that has so much to contribute to this ailing world. I am so honored that you trusted me with your hearts and stories. You have taught me deep lessons around resiliency, authenticity, and belonging. I dedicate this book to you and those young people out there, ready and willing to come closer to their Light.

My spiritual guides, ancestors, and above all to Source, which tasked me to be a vehicle of this beautiful work.

Thank you.

About the Author

© Rhythm Krishna Mohan

Urana Jackson's work with young people and their families has spanned more than twenty years. Born and raised in Los Angeles, California, and now settled in the San Francisco Bay Area, she received her master's degree in Counseling Psychology from Pacifica Graduate Institute in 2005. Urana has created and facilitated social-emotional youth development curricula for various agencies and institutions in the Bay Area, as well as worked as an educator and mental health clinician in public schools and the private sector. She conducts presentations and trainings for schools on incorporating innovative mental health practices and integrating spirituality into social-emotional learning. She leads workshops for adolescent girls based on the curriculum featured in *Girls Rising*. In addition, Urana has a private counseling practice in Napa and Oakland, working primarily with girls and women ages twelve to thirty-five. She is also a creative agent, and her longtime personal meditation practice and involvement in the Native American spiritual community has influenced her work tremendously.

PARALLAX PRESS

Parallax Press is a nonprofit publisher, founded and inspired by Zen Master Thich Nhat Hanh. We publish books on mindfulness in daily life and are committed to making these teachings accessible to everyone and preserving them for future generations. We do this work to alleviate suffering and contribute to a more just and joyful world.

For a copy of the catalog, please contact:

Parallax Press
P.O. Box 7355
Berkeley, CA 94707
parallax.org

RELATED TITLES FROM PARALLAX PRESS

Awakening Joy James Baraz and Shoshana Alexander

Awakening Joy for Kids James Baraz and Michele Lilyanna

Beginning Anew Sr. Chan Khong

Child's Mind Christopher Willard

Dharma, Color, and Culture Hilda Gutierrez Baldoquin

Everybody Present Nikolaj Flor Rotne and Didde Flor Rotne

Happiness Thich Nhat Hanh

Healing Sr. Dang Nghiem

The Mindful Athlete George Mumford

Not Quite Nirvana Rachel Neumann

A Pebble for Your Pocket Thich Nhat Hanh

Planting Seeds Thich Nhat Hanh and the Plum Village Community

Reconciliation Thich Nhat Hanh

Solid Ground Sylvia Boorstein, Norman Fischer, Tsoknyi Rinpoche

Teach, Breathe, Learn Meena Srinivasan

Together We Are One Thich Nhat Hanh